LIVE
WELL
DIE
BROKE

TONY WALKER

ISBN: 978-1-7344267-0-0

Library of Congress Control Number: 2019920966

Printed in Louisville, Kentucky by WorryFree, Inc.

Mailbox Money is a registered trademark of Tony Walker Financial, Inc. and is used here with permission.

Live Well, Die Broke is a trademark of WorryFree, Inc.

The publisher has strived to be as accurate and complete as possible in the creation of this book.

This book is not intended for use as a source of legal, business, accounting, or financial advice. All readers are advised to seek services of competent professionals in legal, business, accounting, and financial fields.

In practical advice books, as in anything else in life, there are no guarantees of income made. Readers are cautioned to rely on their own judgment about their individual circumstances and to act accordingly.

The advice and strategies found within may not be suitable for every situation. This work is sold with the understanding that neither the author nor the publisher is held responsible for the results accrued from the advice in this book.

While all attempts have been made to verify information provided for this publication, the publisher assumes no responsibility for errors, omissions, or contrary interpretation of the subject matter herein.

For more information or for bulk book orders, visit www.LiveWellDieBroke.com.

DEDICATION

This book is dedicated to Savers who have worked hard, saved hard and deep-down, have one simple goal in mind: to use and enjoy the money they have worked so hard to save.

It is also dedicated to all of my family who, collectively, helped create in me a true appreciation for life (and death) and the joys that come from making money, saving money and enjoying money. I've learned from them that whether you have a little or a lot, you can still enjoy life.

Finally, this book is dedicated to all financial professionals and companies who understand the mind of the Saver and strive to assist them in not outliving their money by providing Mailbox Money® for life.

Acknowledgements

A special 'thank you' first goes out to all of the thousands of clients and prospective clients who, over the past 35 years, trusted me with their most personal finances and life goals and all the worries that accompany the hopes and dreams for retirement. Their "real-life" views on money, life and death have helped to shape the unique perspective needed to complete this work.

To all my family listed within the pages of this book. You will never know how much I appreciate and love you for who you are; especially my wife Susan, who has always been so supportive in my life's work and who, years ago, was willing to work nights as a nurse and sleep in a closet in order to provide me the necessary time to get my business off the ground.

To three of my Saver clients, Jill Everett, Theresa Murphy, and Carlos Tutwiler, who took a great deal of time proofreading the manuscript and providing valuable insight on how to make this book even better.

And finally, special thanks to the staff at Worry-Free Productions – Aaron, Gina, Trey and Megan, who sacrificed time from their normal work duties to help make this book a reality; to Kevin Anderson and Associates, who assisted in the editing and formation of the story behind the work; Diana M. Needham, who brought needed expertise in the art of publishing and "launching" a digital book in the 21st century; and Rhonda Harshfield, who brought new life to some old photos allowing a better representation of my past in order to explain the future.

TABLE OF CONTENTS

The greatest use of life is to spend it for something that will outlast it.

— William James

PREFACE

As a retirement planning specialist, whenever I host one of my workshops I begin by talking about my granddad, Bill Hardin. Granddad was born in 1914 and graduated from high school in 1932. College wasn't in the cards for him because he was a young man living in the midst of the Great Depression, a time when most people were concerned with putting food on the table and surviving rather than achieving their higher-education goals. In rural Kentucky, putting food on the table meant hunting, fishing, and growing your own food. This method of survival was paramount given that the unemployment rate at this time was 22 percent.

When the local phone company offered my granddad a job climbing telephone poles, he jumped from the soup-kitchen line onto a BellSouth telephone pole. Granddad knew you didn't get very many opportunities handed to you in life, and you had to take every offer in order to survive. With one in four adults unemployed at the time, Granddad was just grateful to get a job. He knew that if he worked hard for the phone company and kept his nose clean, the phone company would eventually reward him for all of his years of service in the form of a pension: a regular payment that would arrive in his mailbox each and every month for the rest of his life. Granddad called it Mailbox Money®, and it was derived from an investment fund that BellSouth contributed to throughout his employment.

True to the word of the phone company, in 1978 Granddad retired and began receiving his Mailbox Money. This, along with his monthly Social Security check, ensured that he and his beloved wife and my grandmother, Hazel, would enjoy a lifetime of guaranteed income. No matter how long they might live, they would never run out of money. Thanks to the indelible memories of the Great Depression, people in Granddad's day hated the thought of being in debt; layaway was about the closest thing to it, as people usually had zero debt and certainly never owned a credit card. Their philosophy was to only borrow money if they could pay it back from funds already in their bank account. The security from my granddad's pension, his Social Security, and having no debt allowed him to be worry-free about money. All he had to do was spend less than what was showing up each month in the mailbox, and he and Hazel would be fine.

In this way, saving and spending money was very simple for Granddad. For people of Granddad's generation, all of their health insurance costs during retirement were covered by their former employer. Since Granddad was a former employee of the phone company, he even got free long-distance phone service, a huge perk back in the 1970s. Granddad understood the value of a dollar. He didn't have a financial advisor because he didn't need one. There was no such thing as a 401(k) plan, and since most people feared another stock market crash, they would never consider risking their hard-earned money in something they couldn't explain and certainly couldn't understand. For these reasons, Granddad found the thought of putting money in the stock market ludicrous.

Today, 401(k)s have rapidly replaced pensions, leaving most Americans without Mailbox Money. Wall Street has infiltrated Main Street via the 401(k), and has taken the safety, security, and Mailbox Money away from hardworking Americans. This is why so many people are worried about what will happen when they finally retire from their jobs. Recent surveys reflect that Americans' greatest financial fear is running out of money, which was never a fear for Granddad. In contrast, memories of 401(k) accounts rapidly losing value and depleting during the 2008 recession still run strong with most Americans. Even millennials who weren't in the job market remember their parents' fretting over retirement. Much as the Great Depression made its mark on Granddad, the 2008 recession has marked many people today with a fear of not receiving their own version of Mailbox Money.

The idea of maxing out your 401(k) and having all of this money, and feeling that you aren't saving enough, are issues Granddad never had to worry about. The reduction and elimination of pensions has increased worry in a new generation of Savers. Ironically, a buddy of mine recently retired from AT&T; most of his money is in a 401(k). He has a small pension, but guess which one he's worried about? The 401(k), which is completely invested in the stock market. "I don't want to lose it," he told me.

Incidentally, it's ironic that as I'm putting the finishing touches on this book and recognizing that Savers had been forced to replace their beloved mailbox money with risky investments found within the 401K plan, Congress recently passed a bill referred to as the Secure Act. This new law enables most 401K plans to now offer annuities. Why annuities? Because annuities are the only contractual financial investments that can provide Mailbox Money, which is good news for Savers who are currently worried about running out of money. With annuities soon to be offered in their 401K plans, their fears of running out of money will be eliminated.

My granddad's story about his relationship with money is different than my own. I spent a great deal of my childhood and teenage years around Granddad. I admired his work ethic and ability to think pragmatically about money. Yet, as much as I admired him, I always recognized that we were wired differently when it came to our views on work and retirement. I probably wouldn't have worked at BellSouth for as long as my granddad did because an entrepreneurial spirit was just as strong in me as Granddad's grab-any-and-every-opportunity mentality was in him. Being "my own boss" is entrenched in my stories of growing up. For instance, at eight years old, while growing up in Lexington, Kentucky, I would go to the grocery store with my mom. She would let me return the Coke bottles we had accumulated (back in the 1960s, you'd receive two cents for each Coke bottle you returned). I'd then take that money and walk next door to the Ben Franklin five-and-dime to buy penny candy. Then I'd go home and sell my penny candy for two cents to the other kids. I'd turn a twelve-cent investment into twenty-four cents. Not bad! Clearly, I've always been a natural entrepreneur interested in starting my own businesses. Today, as an independent financial advisor who, over the past 35 years has met with more than 15,000 Savers, I still enjoy helping others worry less about money.

I've also always been true to my word. I was taught three things: do what you say you are going to do, follow through, and don't give up or stop trying. I have always participated in the sales process with excitement and new ideas, and taking calculated risks when it came to business endeavors always sparked an electric feeling within me. There was power and creativity in encouraging people to try things, and not necessarily be bound by what everyone else was doing. All of these feelings were very different from Granddad's, whom I admired and loved all the same.

My mom once told me if Granddad had been the product of a generation that didn't endure the Great Depression, he would have likely been an entrepreneur like me. He had several patents to his name, but he never did anything with them. I guess the thought of leaving the security of his job with BellSouth and trying to pursue them was too great a risk. He was from a generation that feared scarcity and valued dependability above all else, these conditions preventing people who had to focus on surviving their surroundings from taking chances.

It wasn't just my granddad who had it tough. My grandmother was one of five kids, raised by a single mom who was left with one option: get out and find work—any kind of work—to make sure she could keep her five kids fed and clothed. This survival mindset was what influenced an entire generation to do whatever it took to work hard and take care of a family. The idea of having Mailbox Money was icing on the cake.

Through these stories, I've learned how money transcends bank accounts and infiltrates not only our thinking, but the generational money stories running through our families. I relate to these stories, which drives my desire to help people—Savers like Granddad—who simply have as their life's mission to work hard so they can achieve financial freedom. Ultimately, my clients know why I believe passionately in the concept of Mailbox Money for life, and why having an income that you can never outlive is crucial for a worry-free retirement.

The philosophy of living well and dying broke is to use and enjoy your money while you can without fearing it will one day run out. Granddad may not have been a whiz about money, but he and his generation understood the simplicity of this concept and wanted to be sure that risk and uncertainty would be the furthest things from their minds. For them, it was all about enjoying the fruits of their labor. The problem is that in the current financial world, Wall Street has successfully instilled risk and uncertainty in the minds of hardworking Savers, convincing them that the only way to make it in retirement is to risk it in the stock market and hang in there when the bad times come, which they will. Their message is one of hanging on to your money because, as they put it, "You'll never know when you might need it." Well, of course they're going to tell you not to spend your own money! The longer you leave it with them, the longer you wait to enjoy it, and the more they make on your money.

You see, financial institutions have a vested interest in you not spending your money. They don't care for the simple notion of Mailbox Money, because this takes the control from them and gives it to you. I, however, want everyone to think about the potential of Mailbox Money in today's economy, and to think about their retirement funds in a way that serves their current goals and dreams. Stockpiling money for the sake of security is no longer the only option. There is a better way, the way of working hard, saving hard, and using and enjoying your money before it's too late.

While Granddad and I have different views on money, he influenced what I would go on to do with my life. As I've talked to thousands of people, I've always kept Granddad in mind and asked the question: How could this man who survived the Great Depression live on so little? Clearly, Granddad was a Saver, not an investor or speculator, but how can people of the generation after Granddad's, my parents' generation, then my generation, and then my children's generation, take his lessons to heart when the world has changed so much? Is Mailbox Money still a possibility for retirees?

People in the last fifty years have likely not experienced the same levels of poverty and financial despair as people did during the Great Depression. And yet, there's still a great deal of uncertainty in the world. After all, nobody anticipated what was going to happen in 1928 when the bottom suddenly fell out. This could happen again in the same unexpected way. As a planner, I try to be realistic, so my clients can relate to their own money like Granddad did to his by living beneath your means and being realistic about your money. In other words: Live Well, Die Broke.

In this book, I share my personal life story with money and how it shaped my passion for guiding people to find their own version of Mailbox Money. Granddad's generation and every generation thereafter have their own challenges and opportunities, ones that interconnect and influence one another. The values I hold about money are not the ones my children hold, as I watch them take on the same skepticism about 401(k)s and the stock market as my Granddad did two generations ago.

Through my family's history and my own story, I'll answer the question: Can you really live well and die broke? You'll see how Mailbox Money is a golden concept for every generation. You'll learn how to build a survivalist attitude toward your money and still honor your desire to spend your hard-earned dollars while you're still able to do so. Granddad died broke, yet was able to live a great life. His kids loved him all the same, and it didn't matter to them that he didn't leave behind a bunch of money. You may not have anything to leave, but you'll be able to live well on your money and make the most of what you're earning. Granddad was able to enjoy life, pulling this off without taking any risk. And you can, too.

Keeping the legacy of my Granddad alive in the minds of the people I've helped has eased the worries of Savers. My job of having them worry less about money has improved their lives and indeed my own, allowing a sense of perspective to prevail over stock-piling dollars because we've been told we need to have a certain amount in retirement or we'll run out. As the great writer Charles Spurgeon once said, "It is bad to see our money become a runaway servant and leave us, but it would be worse to have it stop with us and become our master." Our goal in life is to master our money. The way to do this is to simplify things in such a way that you know what you have and how you're going to use it, enjoy it, and protect it without worrying about how much is going to be left when you die. I hope this book allows you to explore this concept of living well and dying broke. I trust you'll see the wisdom of Granddad's generation and their love and understanding of Mailbox Money for life. His money story, and my other family members' money stories, led me closer to my own story.

Before I get too far ahead of myself, let me share one of my favorite terms to describe individuals who are ready to retire and enjoy their money, but feel guilty about doing just that. I call it the Guilt-Trip Gospel, and I have seen countless people follow it. At the end of every chapter in this book, you'll find a take-away where I offer my thoughts on how my generational story can help you stay worry-free in retirement. By learning from my family's stories and my personal perspective on money, which has come from working in the financial trenches for over thirty-five years, and includes conducting thousands of interviews with Savers, I'm hoping you will ignore the Guilt-Trip Gospel and start living well in retirement.

Chapter 1

GOING, GOING, (NOT REALLY) GONE

"Going once, going twice . . . sold!" shouted the auctioneer.

Sadly, with the death of my Granddad and his beloved Mailbox Money, all that was left were the memories and a vacant house in Troy, Kentucky. A house that represented not only the quality time Mom and all of us spent there, but, just as importantly, represented that Granddad's years of work had come to an official end. Mom, along with Granddad's son (my Uncle Eddie), would be left to divide what was left of Granddad's life's work, a dilapidated house in Troy, Kentucky that just sold at auction for a whopping $85,000.

This house was more than a modest home in "the country," as we used to call it. This house was, as my Uncle Eddie liked to say, "in the land of do-as-you-please." It was our family's retreat, always tranquil, predictable, and relaxing. There was always something good to eat there, too. The thought of someone else buying this house was almost too much; it was a sad

2 Live Well Die Broke

day, indeed. And as for Granddad's life work, he and his faithful wife Hazel truly did die broke.

But for Mom, what she would inherit from her parents was irrelevant. It may have been nice for my mom to inherit some money, sure, but even if she had, I don't think it would have made her any happier, and she probably wouldn't have spent it on anything in particular. It wasn't about the money.

Granddad was born in 1914. He graduated from high school in 1932, smack-dab in the Great Depression, which had started in 1929. During the Great Depression, as mentioned in the Preface, Granddad, Grandma Hazel, and the rest of the Greatest Generation would do anything to survive, not making any moves they deemed too risky. This way of living and thinking was passed on to their children, my mom and my father, and then on to their children, me and my brother. You see, much of what we learn about money and life comes from our parents. Mom and Dad constantly heard stories about the Great Depression and how tough it was to make and save money. Granddad's generation didn't have money to invest, so their only hope was their employer-provided pension plans, which would turn into Mailbox Money when Granddad retired. With that said, there was no "financial planning" going on in the households of my grandparents and parents. As was the way with most people in those days, Grandma Hazel did everything at home to be sure Granddad could focus on work. She supported Granddad when BellSouth offered his telephone-pole climbing gig back in 1932, when unemployment was at 22 percent. From that point forward, Grandma manned the household and Granddad never stopped working until 1978, when he received his pension from the company. Granddad found security in working at the same company for over forty years, which would become an unheard-of feat by the time the gavel was coming down on his old house. At that time, staying loyal to your employer was common practice, and was rewarded with benefits and a pension.

Sentimentality and survival meant something else, too; it meant my grandparents held on to certain things that may not have served them in the present, particularly when it came to money and that magical goal of retirement. I wondered where this desire came from, aside from the technical fact that retirement was created to encourage an older workforce to step aside and make room for a younger one. Instead, I spent a lot of time with Granddad learning about his unique generational perspective. From his stories, I learned that employers were masters at waving the magic carrot of security in front of you. BellSouth encouraged Granddad to keep working with them because, they reminded him, by working hard and keeping his nose clean, and remaining loyal to the company, one day he would start receiving that coveted Mailbox Money.

Even if company loyalty is no longer the key to job or life security, we have different carrots dangled in front of us to encourage us to stay on the corporate wheel. For example, you may have caught yourself saying if you work five more years, you'll qualify for a certain level of assurance that you'll retire at a certain age, or you'll reach a certain number in your retirement account you've calculated in your mind, or that someone else (usually the company managing your 401(k) money, which doesn't want you to retire and start enjoying your money) tells you that you must have in order to retire.

In reality, it's worth considering the risk/reward scenario of staying in a job that may not fuel your passion, but has a benefit like a pension. There are still a few jobs out there offering pensions and, while I understand the desire to keep working so the pension will continue to grow, one must also consider the fact that the pension you are working so hard to receive will one day die with you. You can't pass that pension off at death, but, then again, that may not be so bad since you'll at least be guaranteed Mailbox Money for life. Here's the million-dollar question: Will staying in your current job for X number of additional years mean you limit the things you really want to do in life? In other words, if you keep working longer so you can stockpile more money in either your pension or 401(k) plan, then you will actually put off doing the things you might want to do at a time in your life when you can actually do them.

Recently a seventy-four-year-old gentleman we'll call Dave set up an appointment to see me. Some five years prior to this meeting, he had met with me to try and understand my thinking about him and his wife spending more of their money. Dave never became a client, so when he came back in, I had to ask why. The conversation went something like this:

"So, Dave, what brings you back in after all these years?" I inquired.

"Well, Tony, I have to admit that some five years ago when I first met you, I was taken aback by your suggestion that my wife and I should start spending more of our money, before we couldn't due to health issues or other circumstances."

"So did you?" I asked.

"No, we didn't."

"May I ask why?"

"Well, to be honest, I was afraid to spend it," Dave said. "I mean, I've worked my butt off to save this money for retirement. I always feared running out of money or going into a nursing home or whatever, but now, at the age of seventy-four, I'm finding out what you told me would happen . . . we just are not spending that much money."

"So what's happening to your money?" I asked.

"Oh, the money just keeps growing and growing," said Dave with a sigh. "In fact, I don't even know what to do with it. When we last met, we were thinking of doing a lot of travel one day, but now with her blindness, we can't."

"I'm sorry to hear that. How has that affected your lifestyle?"

"Well, when we last met, we were doing quite a bit of travel, but now with her blindness, we just don't travel anymore."

This follow-up conversation with Dave was a real-life example of what can happen when you continue to stockpile your money instead of enjoying it while you can. While I couldn't turn back the clock on the years to a time when Dave's wife was in better health, I could use it as a teaching moment for those who are asking the same questions Dave did five years ago. Being prudent in this way with your money, it seems, isn't always prudent for your life.

How about you? Are you spending time away from things you truly enjoy doing? While my grand-dad may have seemed prudent, he also didn't pursue his true passion of inventing things that could truly have benefitted more people and possibly provided a better way of life for Grandma Hazel and himself. He could have easily made the decision to set off on an entrepreneurial venture. As I noted earlier, with a keen understanding of engineering and a few patents to his name, Granddad could have taken a chance and gone for it. But he never did. Why? He most likely chose security over risk when it came to making money. A lot of people from my Granddad's generation were intuitively scared of another Great Depression happening in their lifetime, so they created a self-fulfilling prophecy of scarcity. They felt leaving their company would lead to poverty, and therefore they never nurtured the other aspects and potential passions of their lives. One quote can sum up Granddad's experience when it comes to staying with a company, and Mom's later reticence to sell the house and use the proceeds how she wished: "Money can certainly help you get the things you want. The problem is that money can't always help you *keep* the things you want."

In the eyes of my family and me, Granddad's house had to go. He and the memories associated with it were gone. The richest man the world has ever known, King Solomon, summarized his life this way: "Thus I hated all the fruit of my labor for which I had labored under the sun, for I must leave it to the man who will come after me." In Granddad's case, he would never have dreamed that leaving a modest home in "the country"—which was the only asset he left since his Mailbox Money had died with him—would create such an emotional burden for his daughter.

Speaking of King Solomon, the Bible is full of wisdom about money and how we worry about it. The issue of how much is enough is always a question my clients ask me. Jesus knew the heart of man—the question of how much is enough, and how much we should "store up" for the future. He shared an interesting parable about a man who was very wealthy, but who, despite having enough, chose to continue to build more and more barns in order to store it up. Yet, Jesus reminds us of the reality that our time on earth could end in a moment's notice, and all that we have will remain for others to deal with. As the old saying goes, "You really can't take it with you!"

What I have learned about money is that it's a commodity—a tool that allows us to buy the things we need (food, clothing, and a roof over our head) and also the things we want (services or products we don't actually need and are in excess of the basics). For instance, like Granddad, all of us only need a modest home in the country, but some of us (yours truly included) choose to live in a nicer home in a gated community. There's no right or wrong answer here. What we want is different from what others might want.

However, a funny thing happens as we get older—the "wants" become less exciting and we tend to creep back into the "needs." I see this with many, many clients as they grow older. The wisdom of "Why in the world have I spent so much of my life building bigger barns when a modest home in the country would have been just fine?" begins to set in. A seventy-year-old client of mine felt worn out from doing all of this financial planning, and now, as he had reached retirement age, he and his wife didn't seem to really need it. What they thought they would need for the things they thought they would want turned out to be a futile effort.

Regardless of what you have or what you might want, know that there is no real lasting value in money. It is simply a tool to be used and enjoyed, and that's it. If the money is stored in a bigger barn when you die, it's no longer in your control but in the control of someone else who may or may not use and enjoy it the way you did. In fact, as you will discover as you read this book, one day those bigger barns may become a curse for your loved ones. This is what is meant by Live Well, Die Broke. We all live a certain way, but in the end we all die broke. You and I will die, and what we have, no matter how big our barns might be, will go to someone else. In the case of my granddad, his life was summed up with an old house at auction and a constant source of Mailbox Money that came to an end. A well-funded retirement account is great, but it may not keep you safe from a life that's not been fully examined and explored.

Mom desperately wanted to keep the old house and the associated memories alive. Me? I heard a different story that gave me a new perspective on her feelings. A current financial client of mine owned five cars, and as I was visiting with him and his wife, I asked her about her husband's many cars. Sitting together, the conversation between this couple went something like this:

"He can't drive all five of them, and it is about time he seriously thinks about selling one or two," she said.

"I can't sell any of these cars!" he said. "They're worth at least $125,000."

"Exactly," she said. "I'd like to have $125,000 in the bank so we can spend it, rather than have it sitting in your garage where we can't."

"But, honey, we've talked about this before. I have too much invested in these babies. You know how much I love to polish them and drive them around. I've got my life's work in them."

You see, this man valued the cars and the memories they provided more than the thought of seeing someone else enjoy his passion and life's work. Money to him meant nothing in comparison to these five cars. I can understand this. As an advisor, the solution to having more money to spend and enjoy was simple—sell the darn cars! But, to him, to sell the cars would have been akin to selling a part of himself. He just couldn't do that. To him, it wasn't about the money.

in the same way, it didn't make sense for Mom to struggle so much with the thought of letting go of Granddad's home. But it made sense to her based on her money story, family memories, and values. She treasured how we spent time together in that home as a family during the good and the bad seasons. This idea of prioritizing experiences over money would have interesting consequences for Mom. As we'll see in Chapter 2, her money story would become entwined with the story of a man named Dick Walker, her future husband and my dad.

Dad had a very different view of money. As we'll see in the next chapter, my parents' relationship with their funds, how they worked to earn those funds, and what they did once they had money in the bank would influence my budding money story.

Live Well, Die Broke Takeaway #1:
Choose to live well while you can.

Have you ever considered how much money you'll leave behind when you die? Have you ever inherited money? When it comes to what's left when we die, what looks like one person's financial burden may be another's financial passion or source of joy. Retiring with a sack of money in the bank is not always the best remedy for a smooth, worry-free retirement.

Instead, consider what was important to my grandparents in their own retirement years, and what was left after they died. Mom wanted to keep the house filled with her love for her family for years and years. No right or wrong answers here; just heavy-duty decisions that will one day face us all. In the end, we will all die broke. The question is how we will choose to live well while we can. Do you have a regular way to collect a check when you retire, Mailbox Money as Granddad used to call it? If not, why not? Are you working hard to build bigger barns with no clue as to who will get what when you die, or worse yet, no way of knowing how they will handle what you leave them?

In this serious dilemma, we all have our own choices to make. They're just different ways, beyond stockpiling money, of approaching a nontraditional retirement.

Chapter 2

THE TRUE MEANING OF A TWENTY-DOLLAR BILL—"IT'S NOT ABOUT THE MONEY"

My dad, Dick Walker, may have been working in social services for all of his life, but he was a born salesman. As the saying goes, he could sell ice to an Eskimo. Gifted with the art of persuasion and good looks, he could convince anyone to buy or do just about anything. As a gifted high-school saxophone player in the 1950s, Dad was awarded a partial scholarship to play in the marching band at the University of Kentucky (UK). Luckily for Dad, this was during famed coach Bear Bryant's days at UK, where "The Bear" took the UK football team to two different bowl games – a big deal back then. Dad used to tell people he played for Bear Bryant in two different Bowl Games. As people impressively nodded in surprise, Dad never told them that he'd meant "played in the marching band" – not on the football team. I always thought that was funny.

Besides working part time as a dorm monitor and finding time to play in the UK marching band, Dad also used his wit and good charm to talk the powers that be at UK into allowing him to teach a bowling class. Dad had little knowledge of bowling but that didn't matter. He had a knack for having fun with people, cutting up, and acting like he knew what he was talking about, confidently going about his business teaching students as if he did. It didn't matter what it was; it could have been badminton, and he would have gone for it. He was a natural salesman, and would raise his hand for any fun challenge.

This was what many people who took his class remembered him for. The legacy of my dad's bowling class had an impact on his students. Shortly after my father's death in 1996, a gentleman in my hometown who was a student in my dad's bowling class at UK, told me, "the only 100 I made at UK was the 100 I scored in your dad's bowling class."

Dad would have thought that pretty funny.

Newfound raving fans of bowling and scoring an easy A in bowling weren't the only results of Dad's happy-go-lucky approach to life and money. He also met Mom, a freshman who, along with one of her friends, took his bowling class as an elective. At first she thought Dad was cocky, but soon she fell for his charm and good looks. Shortly thereafter, they got married and had my brother Marty, then me. Keep in mind that back in the fifties, getting married right out of college was expected, even encouraged, especially if you were a young woman. It's been said that back then, many young women went to college, not necessarily to get a good education but to find a good man. Their goal was the "MRS" degree, an antiquated term for those attending university to find a husband. They often had a real reason beyond this superficial term, which was indicative of the times: women my mom's age were often eager to start living their lives apart from their families. They wanted to have their own homes, but didn't have the necessary financial means. For these women, marriage was both a financially viable and socially acceptable way of leaving their childhood homes.

My decent lower-middle-class upbringing with my parents meant we were able to survive on my dad's small salary. The house I grew up in—the same home my mother still enjoys today—was a basic home built shortly after World War II. You know the type: brick, three small bedrooms, a little bathroom (that's right, kids; back then, everyone shared one bathroom!), and a driveway about six feet wide with a small detached wooden garage at the end. Why only a six-foot-wide driveway? Because in those days, most families, including ours, only had one car because that was all most could afford.

Dad worked as a social worker, and was the executive director of a small group home for children. Mom stayed at home and took care of us. With Dad's meager salary, we were able to afford one car that got us to and from the grocery store and the other places we needed to go. I remember riding with my mom as she sometimes dropped Dad off at work on those days when she needed the car to run errands. Looking back, those were very simple times—good times in many ways, because you didn't have "multiple" things to worry about. One car—one worry. Three cars—three worries. One car—a one-car garage to keep it in. Three cars—you need a three-car garage to keep them in. One car—only one set of tires every 40,000 miles. Three cars—three sets of tires every 40,000 miles.

Get the picture?

You see, money is a funny thing. The more you have, the more you want. In reality, if you so choose, the more you have, the less you need. A great quote I read once, related to our wants and needs, goes something like this: "A luxury once enjoyed soon becomes a necessity." Basically, in those early days of my childhood and my parents' marriage, planning for retirement still wasn't in the picture; we had the necessities and didn't struggle as much as Granddad did during the Great Depression. The idea of "planning for the future" was the furthest thing from my parents' financial planning, and in fact didn't emerge as a mainstream idea until later in the seventies. Unlike my granddad, who was fortunate enough to work for a big company and get his Mailbox Money in retirement, my dad was not offered a pension. There was nothing out there—no safety net in place—to catch him when he retired. It was up to him to plan for his own retirement and, unfortunately, my dad was no planner.

Why didn't Dad worry about money and retirement? One possible reason was that he didn't really have to. His parents didn't know anything about saving money or retirement, either. Growing up in the mining community of Drakesboro, Kentucky, Dad's introduction to living life was the day-to-day grind of a meager home attached to the back of a general store—a small country store that catered to the local coal miners that his father ran. His father's wife, Granny Walker, was a stay-at-home mom and later a schoolteacher.

My mom, who was recently recounting her experience of the first time Dad took her to the big city of Drakesboro to meet his parents, said she could not believe the living conditions and how hard Granny Walker worked to take care of the household while Granddad Walker hung out at the country store selling the odds and ends the coal miners might need.

I guess when you compare my lifestyle as a kid, Dad must have thought with a nice little home in Lexington, one nice car, and a fairly cushy job running a children's home, he had all that he needed. All he had to do was work his nine-to-five job and play sax in his dance band on weekends for some spare change. What more was there to worry about?

Since my father's dad didn't have a pension, they just learned to live paycheck to paycheck. That's how Dad grew up and that's how he continued to think of money. You work hard and you get paid, and you spend that money on whatever is needed for that day. As a teenager, Dad delivered ice to the locals who needed it for their "ice chests," which people used until refrigerators became a common household appliance. Back then, that's how you made money. As you became an adult, you found something to do that would pay you a steady paycheck, and you worked.

In general, though, Dad's generation was the first that actually made more money than their parents. For them, stockpiling money, as I mentioned in the previous chapter, was starting to become one of the main ways people lived well into retirement, even if Dad wasn't a part of that group. You see, while Dad was full of good looks, smarts, and a knack for being good with people, he was terrible with money. It affected his marriage to my mother. As a kid, I can remember hearing them argue over money—or, shall I say, the lack thereof.

To combat the issue of not having enough money, Dad, who was a talented saxophone player, along with Mom, an excellent piano player, decided to play "dance jobs" on the weekends. This was the only financial relief they had to what was a basic low-paying job in social services. Recently, I asked Mom if she enjoyed all of those late-night weekends in Lexington, playing at local nightclubs and country clubs while Marty and I stayed home with the babysitter, to which she responded, "I hated every minute of it."

The retirement age of sixty-five was introduced by German Chancellor Otto von Bismarck in 1883. Bismarck was trying to sway public opinion against Marxists, and offered that anyone over the age of sixty-five could retire and the state would pay a pension. In 1950, the life expectancy of an American was 68.14 years old. Today, the life expectancy of an American is 78.87 years, and 19 percent of people 65 and older are working full- or part-time. Retirement and the magical age of calling it quits at sixty-five was a concept brought about by politicians who in 1932 needed to follow Bismarck's idea of getting older workers off the assembly line to make room for younger ones. The way to do this was by offering them free retirement income called social security.

Despite changing working and social landscapes, retirement is still seen as what happens after you're done working for many years. In one survey, 6 out of 10 workers said they felt confident or somewhat confident about being able to enjoy the kind of retirement they wanted. Among millennials, 63 percent preferred cash to stocks or mutual funds for retirement savings.

Even if retirement seems like a worthwhile goal, it may be detrimental to a retiree's mental health. The

Mental Health Foundation claimed that 1 in 5 present-day retirees suffers from depression. The study further claimed there was a 40-percent increase in the chance of developing depression after retirement. If you've done one thing for most of your life and you're unable to do it anymore, you're going to need to find new uses of your time. Otherwise, when hobbies aren't enough to keep your mind going, you may feel lost and unable to steer a new course.

Throughout my parents' marriage, though, money was always an issue. My mom later told me what I'd assumed all along, that my dad was terrible with money. He didn't understand how to use it, save it, or invest it. Without knowing how to plan for the future, the two of them did their best to work hard and hope for the best. Neither ever talked about the R-word: retirement.

Although they cared for each other, my parents were not a match. After thirteen years of marriage, in 1970 they divorced. This compelled my mom, who didn't have a college education, to take a nine-to-five insurance job as a clerical assistant making minimum wage. On top of that, she still had to take care of the household and Marty and me. A tough task for a woman in the seventies without a support system.

Funny story about my dad following his divorce from Mom. I guess to try to stay connected to me and Marty, Dad would swing by on weekends to take us out for a few hours—you know, to do guy things.

Occasionally, he'd take us to my favorite destination in Lexington, a little golf course kinda place that included a cool Putt-Putt course, a driving range, and a par-three eighteen course, all in the same area. Now keep in mind, not only did my parents have very little money, but my dad was now divorced and paying alimony to my mom. During this period of time, he rented a little makeshift apartment located in the basement of a nice couple's home. I remember the first time I walked into his apartment. With only one small window to let some light in, my dad sarcastically said that he "felt like a little mole living there." I thought the place was awesome.

Anyway, one day, we headed over to the golf complex to play some Putt-Putt, hit some range balls, and then play the par-three course. If you can picture this, the driving range, which was really not that large, butted right up to the first tee box of the par-three course. In an effort to keep errant range balls from flying onto the par-three course, they had erected a fairly tall fence that separated the area where people drove range balls from those who were trying to play golf on the par-three course. Nevertheless, range balls were always flying over the fence onto the first fairway.

After the three of us "shared" our one bucket of balls, it was off to play the neighboring par-three course. My dad got off his wallet and purchased a very expensive sleeve of three *ACHUSNET* brand golf balls, which, at that time were the priciest balls available. Armed with our three golf balls, we proceeded from the pro shop to the first tee box, a short par-three of only about 100 yards.

As we approached the first tee, Dad told Marty to hit first. As my dad and I stood watching Marty take a few practice swings, Dad hollered out, "Come on, Marty, hit the damn ball!"

So Marty swung with all his might in hopes of getting it to the green some 100 yards away. But instead of hitting it straight toward the green, Marty's ball quickly made a hard-left turn and disappeared over the fence and onto the driving range.

Of course, it would have been dangerous to walk around the fence and onto the driving range to retrieve this brand-new ball, as there were at least twenty people still on the range that were worse than we were. Balls were flying all over the place. Dad, trying to be patient with Marty, calmly told him to hit another one. Keep in mind, we now only had two balls left for three golfers. Well, you guessed it . . . Marty's second shot was worse than the first, as it crossed the fence and disappeared among the hundreds of balls lying on the driving range.

Now what? Three golfers with only one ball left.

My dad was furious and quickly shouted to me: "Okay, Tony, it's your turn!"

I've played a lot of competitive sports, but walking up to that little tee box on this day and not thinking about hitting our last ball over that fence was the most pressure I have ever felt. Luckily, I kept it in play, hitting a decent shot some 20 yards or so in front of the green.

As we walked off the tee box and proceeded to the green, I was wondering how in the world we were going to play with just this one ball when suddenly my Dad said, "Hey boys, pick up some of those range balls and put 'em in your pockets."

You see, while there was an occasional ball that proceeded from the par-three onto the driving range, there were a ton of balls that went from the driving range over the fence and onto the first fairway of the par-three course. Normally, you just walked by the range balls knowing that those were off-limits to golfers. But on this day, with only one ball left and my dad with no more money to run back into the pro shop to buy more, he would, in Dick Walker style, improvise.

As we were picking up range balls and stuffing them into our pockets, Dad grabbed a couple (one for him and one for Marty) and literally threw them up on the green as if nothing had happened. Still playing the ball I just hit, I chipped it onto the green.

Happy to be back in business and armed with plenty of golf balls to last through the round, we walked up to the first green to putt. As the three of us were standing over our balls, a little Jeep, the caged-in kind they used back then so the driver could drive around the range and pick up range balls, came flying around the tall fence separating the driving range from the golf course and onto the par-three course, heading right toward us. As the Jeep slid to a stop just feet from the green, a huge guy who looked to be about twenty-one—picture the late actor John Candy—got out of the Jeep and tugged at his pants to hike them up. He began to walk toward us.

My dad looked up as if he just noticed him, and said in a sarcastic tone, "Whatcha need, tiger?"

The young man responded in a real official-sounding voice, "Excuse me, sir, you wouldn't happen to have any of our range balls, would you?"

My father looked at him, looked at us as we stood with our pockets bulging from the range balls inside, then looked back at him and said, "Man, what would we want with a bunch of range balls . . . we got enough money to buy this place!" Then, he simply looked down and putted. The young man, confused and dismayed, got in his little Jeep and drove back to the driving range to continue picking up range balls.

What's the point of this story, you ask? It's another reminder that it doesn't take a lot of money to build memories. I have a smile on my face whenever I tell that story. It was one of those rare moments with Dad when his carefree attitude toward money became a memory Marty and I still talk about to this day. We were thrilled to be a part of Dad's "on-the-fly" scheme. To me, that was worth more than a lot of money in the bank.

*   *   *

In 1973, my dad took a new position in Bowling Green, KY. In 1975, much to the surprise of friends and family, I picked up stakes and moved to Bowling Green to live with him. I had the gumption to move to a new town, and Bowling Green was considered a really small town compared to Lexington. I had an opportunity to play Babe Ruth baseball there, and since my mom and I weren't getting along too well, I wanted to try something new. Intuitively, I felt like I needed a change. I didn't feel right staying in the same space. Mom was struggling to make it. I was a rowdy teenager. Dad always said, "Nothing stays the same," but I thought change was good. To step out on faith and seize the moment can be a good thing.

Now able to make more of my own money decisions, I had different goals when it came to work, money, and my future. I realized that if I was going to make it in life, it would be up to me. The can-do spirit I was blessed with kept me going. I decided to try to excel at whatever I was going to do. In the end, I feel the divorce actually made me a stronger person and allowed me to experience things I wouldn't have, had my parents stayed married. I learned at a young age there is a silver lining in every circumstance. Who knows, but isn't that what faith is all about?

When I entered college, during the summers I began working odd jobs, including washing dishes at a local restaurant, cooking fried chicken at another, and burying telephone cable (of all things). A college friend of mine who was running his own painting service encouraged me to start my own. I didn't know anything about painting houses, but figured it must beat cooking chicken and burying telephone cable.

So, armed with a 28-foot extension ladder Grand-dad loaned me and a few paintbrushes, Collegiate Painting Services was in business. Here I was, a twenty-year-old college kid confidently walking into the local paint store wearing my "white painter's pants" while all of the older (more mature and with much more experience) painters were sitting there drinking coffee and looking at me as if to say, "Who in the world is this young whippersnapper?" Not to be intimidated by a bunch of experienced painters in a paint store, I would do my best Dick Walker impersonation (you know, the guy who knew nothing about bowling but was able to convince people he did) and talk my way into the paint store giving me the "contractor's price" on all paint and painting supplies.

I loved painting houses and, believe it or not, got very good at it and stayed very busy during college. Heck, the money I made from painting in college allowed me to buy my high-school sweetheart's engagement ring!

Once I managed to work out the pricing deal with the paint store, I had to find some customers whom I could convince to let a college kid start slapping paint on their homes. I started by simply riding around neighborhoods and putting flyers in mailboxes that read, *Help a kid through college, let me paint your house.* Once I got my first job, I placed a sign out in the front yard that simply said COLLEGIATE PAINTING and included my phone number. The calls and the jobs slowly came in, and I was in business! Those few years of being my own boss painting houses and making pretty good money confirmed what I had known from the early days of selling penny candy: I had a way with people, and I worked hard and tried to do right by the customer. These are lessons in business that are still with me today.

My painting business took off from there. For three summers, I was busy painting, and making good money while doing it. I had a knack for showing up on time, being responsible, and being creative about how to market myself. I also harnessed the power of referrals. When people heard I was doing a good job, I'd be recommended for the next job. I also loved the challenge of becoming a better painter and challenging the old guard. My goal was to be as good a painter as the experienced, if not better, at the tender age of twenty.

This kind of spirit was clearly different from my grandparents' and parents'; I was looking to make my own way in the world. Not only did I have a knack for making money with my business skills, but I began to explore my passions. This was something Granddad never did with his patents, and my father only explored minimally himself.

In 1982, after floundering in college for four years, I began to pursue academic opportunities in broadcasting. Along with my major in psychology (which I'd accumulated enough hours for, as a result of all my floundering), I enrolled in the broadcast journalism department at Western Kentucky University. I was the same age Dad was when he taught bowling in college. A job opening pinned to a bulletin board caught my eye: a minimum wage weekend broadcasting job of writing news and spinning records at a 250-watt radio station.

Right away, I called the small-town station and set up an interview with the manager, Henry Stone, a seasoned radio reporter and veteran of the business. From the first interview with Mr. Stone, I could tell he meant business. He was stern but fair, an old-school reporter type who would teach me how to put together a story. After a brief interview with Mr. Stone, I convinced him that I was the man for the job. Much like my dad convincing his school that he could teach bowling, even though he didn't even bowl, I was getting my start with enthusiasm rather than experience.

Henry hired me on the spot, handed me the keys to the studio, and told me to be there on Sunday mornings at 5:30 a.m. "What's happening at that hour?" I asked him. He told me that was when all the preachers and gospel singers came down to the studio and sang live on air. Excited about my first day of work, I arrived at the station at 4:30 a.m., turned on the lights, and set up the radio transmitters as best I could. Then, I heard a knock. I got up from the control board and walked to the front door. Standing on the front-porch stoop were three African-American women, the Soul Sister Trio, dressed in their Sunday best and featuring perfectly applied makeup. I realized this wasn't their first rodeo as they said hello and walked right past me, heading for the studio just across the hall from the control room.

They moved into the dimly lit studio and toward a small piano and a few microphones on stands. They handed me a twenty-dollar bill to cover their 30 minutes of scheduled air- time and off they went, singing the Gospel as if the joy of God had just engulfed them.

I had never seen anything like it; the joy with which these three sisters sang is still burned in my mind. Their passion and desire to sing to others who might be listening made a huge impression on me, a twenty-two-year-old college kid.

While the sisters were still singing passionately live on the air for thirty minutes, I heard another knock at the front door. At this point, not knowing what in the heck was going on, I got up quickly from the studio control board and walked to the door—the three gospel singers still going to town in the other studio. Standing on the front stoop was a gentleman holding a Bible.

I opened the door and asked, "May I help you?"

"Yes," he replied politely. "I'm Pastor Larry." He also handed me a twenty-dollar bill and walked right past me, waiting his turn for the studio to open up. In a few minutes, the sisters were done with their singing and calmly left the studio, and in walked Pastor Larry as I gave him the cue to preach—and, man, did he preach.

I couldn't believe this was my job every Sunday morning. I was a small instrument that allowed others to invest themselves in the lives of others. This experience became a master class for me in my own generational money story: from Granddad seeing money as a means of survival and not pursuing his patents; to Dad not saving and for the most part pursuing his passion for music; to me, a young man with a talent for entrepreneurship and broadcast journalism. The culmination of hard work and passion happening every Sunday morning stirred up a fire in me that has lasted throughout my life.

Why would people put down twenty bucks to sing on the radio? Back in the 1980s, twenty dollars adjusted for inflation would now be sixty-five. That's the price of a decent meal out. That's an electric bill. This was the kind of money the pastor and the singing trio were willing to put down for their passion. People from the outside looking in would have probably thought they were being frivolous. Instead, they were paying for something far more precious than the opportunity to sing on the radio; they were investing in sacred time to do what they loved, even if they were doing it for thirty minutes of airtime at 5:30 a.m. on a Sunday when very few people were listening. It was worth it to them. These folks would come to the station at the crack of dawn, in fact *pay* to be there at the crack of dawn. They clearly had a heart for sharing and communicating, even if, as a money spender, it was the opposite of a money maker. A tiny radio station in Franklin, Kentucky was providing this service for people, and it gave me an appreciation for little radio stations in small towns. This was a big part of communities back then, and it taught me about responsibility. Pastor Larry and the trio were investing in others with their own dollars. And, most importantly, they were using their money instead of stockpiling it.

Although the pastor and trio may not have thought of this explicitly, they intuitively knew the longer you keep money, the less valuable it becomes. It's like a pond with stagnant water. The lesson they taught me became one of the many reasons I would guide people through their own retirement dreams. I was beginning to understand why the financial world never encourages Savers to use and enjoy their money, so that the money can stay locked up inside their 401k plans. In fact, I've learned the financial world doesn't want you to use and enjoy your money. Why? Because if you take it from them, they lose money. It doesn't benefit them to have you use the money while you can.

That's why my job, and the job of every other retirement planning specialist, is to help you clarify what it is you want to do with your money. This is your life and your money, and contrary to what others might tell you, money is only worth what it's worth today. Tomorrow is not guaranteed. Here's the dirty little secret that few understand: over time, your money, if not spent, will become more and more worth less—not more valuable but less valuable. You see, just like the gospel sisters and the pastor, they knew the twenty dollars was better spent and invested in the lives of others now versus later. This leads us to a pretty deep question: What is the purpose of money? What's money really for? This would become a question I would continue to ask throughout my life.

Following my 18 month stint at WFKN radio, I applied to numerous TV stations for a full-time job as a reporter, only to discover that no one in that field needed a 23-year-old aspiring sports caster. In retrospect, I was too impatient to pay my dues, but it was still a great life lesson for me. By God's grace, my training and education in broadcasting allowed me to later host my own TV show for many years. For that, I'm grateful for the journey and the lessons I learned from those twenty-dollar bills that were invested in the lives of others.

Over the years, working and meeting with thousands of people, I've learned that people are wired differently, which impacts their motivations around money. I also realized, as much as I loved him, I wasn't completely like Granddad. I couldn't stay in the same job for my whole life to collect benefits at the end. I also wasn't Dad, who worked as a social worker just to get by with his family and who didn't have a plan for how he would afford to live if he didn't work.

My brother Marty became a social worker and musician, just like Dad. And just like my father, he's really good at both! I, however, wanted to pursue my entrepreneurial interests. I was willing to throw that twenty-dollar bill at whatever might stimulate not only my interests in people and money, but might benefit many others by way of that same spirit. Yet, this could be a risky road. These wouldn't be days like my college days, when I was on my own and painting a few houses. I would eventually marry and have three kids who depended on my ability to provide for them. How much risk would I be willing to take? How was I going to provide for them in a sustainable way? My businesses in high school and college had piqued my interest in entrepreneurship, but would I continue on that path? And how was I going to forge a new path of money when it came to my personal relationships?

Live Well, Die Broke Takeaway #2:
Define your big mission.

What's your twenty-dollar mission? What are you passionate about? While it may not be waking up at 5:30 a.m. and forking over twenty dollars to sing on the radio, I bet you have something in mind that you are truly passionate about. If there's a show you want to see, buy the tickets. If you've always wanted to take the grandkids on an all-expense-paid vacation, get off your wallet and plan it. The greatest regret is usually *not* having the experience instead of having it, so feel free to use your money to fuel your personal passions.

Chapter 3

SUSAN FINALLY COMES OUT OF THE CLOSET

Much like my dad, who met his bride-to-be in college, I would meet my bride-to- be in an educational setting too; in 1976 in the halls of Bowling Green high school. It was 1976 and I'd moved to Bowling Green to attend high school, where my dad lived. I didn't know many people, but my new friend Donnie said, "I've got some- one you need to meet." In the library, which we called the Commons, Donnie brought her over. I didn't know who Susan Moore was, but when I first saw her, I never forgot. There was something about her. Susan's kind smile did me in, and from then on I wanted to know more about her. We took long drives in the car and got to know each other, and dated all through high school. We married in 1983. The entwining of my money story with hers would impact us both, leading to what I like to call money shared in a relationship: "We Money."

We Money are the funds shared between a couple. Even if one person makes more money than the other, We Money all goes into the same pot. It means that neither spouse is allowed to question what the other is spending. To me, in order for a marriage to thrive, it must be based on sound principles of basic money management and trust. There must be clear, simple ground rules on how the money will be spent and invested. Both spouses must be in agreement that, no matter what, all the money is We Money. They have to trust the other person to spend the money as they need, but also respect what the other person in the relationship needs and wants.

As it turns out, the decision for Susan and I to go the We Money route would become a very important aspect of our marriage. When my wife was a child, she watched her dad control all of the family finances. Her mom was a school teacher with little training about money. Susan's father was the opposite. He loved investing and planning and was good at overseeing the family finances. He ran the financial household. It just made good financial sense to let Mr. Moore handle the finances. Because of this experience, Susan looked to me to run the finances when we first got married. But this wasn't at all what I wanted for our marriage. After watching my parents constantly argue about money, I was hell-bent on making sure Susan and I didn't do the same thing. I expressed the two things we *weren't* going to do in our marriage: 1) We were never getting divorced, and 2) All of the money we made would be We Money.

What was Susan's reaction to these pre-marriage vows? She respected my commitment to our marriage and money. She agreed that in order to stay married, we needed to get on and stay on the same page, money-wise. No matter who brought what to the table, we would share it. At the start of our marriage, she was the one who made more money. Years later, I began pulling in the bulk of our money. Regardless of who made what, we threw it all in the same kitty and still do to this day.

The term "We Money" actually comes from my dad, but he didn't mean it in the same way I did. I remember first hearing my dad use this phrase in college. One of my buddies, Chuck, who was engaged to be married soon, had just purchased a little Chevy Chevette. He was so proud of that car and wanted to drive over to our house to show it off. As my dad and I walked out of the house to check out Chuck's new ride, in typical Dick Walker fashion, Dad said, "Hey, nice car, Chuck. Where'd you get it?"

"Well, me and my girlfriend bought it together," said Chuck.

"Oh, okay," my dad said. "That's a *we* car!"

At the time, this just seemed like a typical smart-aleck comment my dad would make about money and marriage. But my perspective on this phrase began to change. My observations of my dad always showed me how his inability to manage money was sometimes vindicated by his ability to throw out one-liners that really did make sense.

After processing Dad's "We Car" comment, it dawned on me that in marriage it's all "We Money." Dad's sarcastic attitude toward sharing money in his marriage was exactly why he and my mom constantly fought about money. In other words, if Dad had taken the We Money approach to his first marriage, the marriage may have lasted. Perhaps Mom and Dad would have even enjoyed playing music together, and Mom wouldn't have felt resentful about it. She wouldn't have had to take that clerical job when they divorced.

Speaking of We Money and divorce, I see in my daily practice quite a few people who are retired or nearing retirement and who are in their second or sometimes third marriage. This concept of We Money can be a little sticky. In fact, when I find out that the married couple I'm meeting with is into their second or third marriage, I always ask the following question: "Do the two of you keep your money separate or is your money We Money?" It's a polite way of trying to find out how they view money, since they each have likely brought their own money into the marriage as opposed to being married to only each other all of their married lives. It gets particularly awkward talking about what happens to "your money" when you die. Does "your money" go to "your kids" by your first marriage, or does it go to your second spouse, with "your money" possibly then going to his or her kids when he or she dies? See the dilemma?

My advice for couples and money—even if they are on their second or third marriage—is talk with someone who is trained to have a conversation about this; the dilemma of how to handle "Your Money" in a "We Money" marriage is a toughie. There's no right or wrong answer, but not talking about it can, over time, lead to more problems and resentment, particularly when one spouse dies. Yes, this is another example of where the Live Well, Die Broke approach to money, life, and divorce can be helpful.

Anyway, I decided to take We Money to heart and make it real. Susan and I were going to respect each other's wishes about what we each did with the money we earned, for better or worse. I would take charge of the money and Susan would trust me to do so in order for her to focus on her job as a nurse and to help raise our three children.

Before I owned my current business as a retirement advisor, I got a job working in property casualty insurance with Susan's dad, Mr. Bill Moore. Mr. Moore's brother was General Hal Moore, played by actor Mel Gibson in the movie *We Were Soldiers*. In that tradition, my father-in-law was the type of person who forged ahead, but I didn't let him intimidate me. He was stern at first, kind of like my old station manager, Henry Stone, but eventually I learned he wasn't that way just for me. Once I got past it, he was a really nice fellow. We got along great. I also learned about his personal story. He'd contracted polio at a young age, so he would have to visit the hot springs in Georgia, as many people did back then, to heal. Because of his polio, he had to set aside one of him dreams of playing college baseball at Notre Dame. At the ripe young age of 18 and armed with a scholarship to do just that, polio had other plans, taking away his chance to play baseball. Against all odds, Mr. Moore continued with his education and graduated from Notre Dame.

By the time I met Mr. Moore, he was wearing braces on his legs and had to walk with the assistance of a cane. Although at times he really struggled to walk, he never complained and continued to work through it, soon becoming a successful businessman thanks to creativity and being there at the right place and time. He bought his business from his boss. It was an independent insurance agency. The owner sold him the business, but Mr. Moore still had to contend with paying interest rates that were going through the roof at that time. To ensure his new business didn't go under on his watch, Mr. Moore had enough gumption and foresight to buy a life insurance policy on the owner; he secured enough life insurance on the owner so if the owner died, Mr. Moore could then use the tax-free proceeds from the policy to pay off the business loan. Unlike Dad, Mr. Moore was a planner.

He always thought of what-ifs, and that's why he was a successful business owner. He was also pragmatic and knew about investments. His foresight to cover his risk of the huge loan he had to repay to the former business owner paid off. The owner who sold the business to Mr. Moore did, in fact, pass away shortly after the purchase. Mr. Moore received the tax-free life insurance and the loan was repaid in full. I remember Mr. Moore telling me that had it not been for the life insurance, he would have had no way to keep the business going. The interest was just too much.

At the time Mr. Moore offered me a job with the insurance company, I was still trying to make it in broadcast journalism. I was selling radio ads and sending the videotapes I self-produced around the United States. But I didn't get any job offers. Mr. Moore must have heard me complaining about not having a job and being unable to earn a living, so he offered me a job working with him in the insurance business. I had to do something, so I went for it.

In June of 1984, Mr. Moore offered me a job with his insurance agency, Bill Moore Insurance. As I worked with him, he stayed tough on me. In fact, I didn't even have a book of business when I came to the agency. I had to create one from scratch. To do this, I would "cold-call" people to try and drum up business. I had no problem with this, as I thought about the days of selling penny candy or talking people into letting me paint their homes. After my first year working hard with Mr. Moore, I almost gave up, but his tough love encouraged me to keep going.

Finally, after focusing more on the planning end of things versus simply just selling insurance, I was ready to strike out on my own, and did so in 1989. I had different goals that I wanted to pursue, but I still needed decent cash flow to keep my household going. I was able to leap toward this goal because my wife kept working as a nurse full-time. This is where the first test of We Money came into play. My business was sucking us dry at first; without Susan, we wouldn't have made it to where we are today. Susan was unconditionally supportive when I would later borrow against our home to keep my business going. This was because she knew my heart and my convictions. She knew I wasn't ever going to give up on my business. I wasn't reckless with my decision-making, but everything always seemed to work out as long as we kept at it.

In those early days, my wife was the main breadwinner while I was getting my business off the ground. There were office and employee bills to pay, along with simply trying to get my own clients. I learned how to cover my business when I was on my own and having to navigate entrepreneurship with a hardworking wife and family. My wife worked twelve-hour night shifts, from 7 p.m. to 7 a.m. By Susan working nights, I could stay with the kids. While I was struggling to start my business, we were able to keep it all going thanks to my wife's steady paycheck. Our secret to a happy, successful marriage and life: We Money.

But it wasn't all smooth sailing, even though we did have this respect for each other and commitment to We Money. At one point, in fact, our finances got so bad that I had to go to Mr. Moore (which was very embarrassing for me) and borrow $25,000 to pay a bunch of bills that had mounted up. Being the practical man that he was, Mr. Moore made me sign a note to be sure I paid him back, with interest. I couldn't wait to get that note paid off as quickly as possible, which I did through building my business and making regular payments. I was set on continuing on my and Susan's We-Money path after handling this matter.

Most of the paychecks may have been coming in from Susan, but we were still committed to We Money, no matter who was making more or less of it. Susan never questioned me about what I'd spend money on, and vice versa. We never made money a priority and never put pressure on how much money we might have or desire to have in the future.

Having We Money meant we both had to pitch in and keep the flow of money coming into our household, especially since we had three kids to support. Susan and I had a routine that might have seemed odd to some, but which worked for us and kept us in tune with our We-Money values. After working a 12-hour shift, Susan would return home around 7:30 a.m., only to retreat to our converted closet where she hoped to get a few hours of sound sleep. With the kids running wild in the household, Susan couldn't sleep during the day. Our bedroom had this huge closet that was away from the hustle and bustle of the rest of the house. When you were inside and shut the door, you could shut out all of the noise. So, we made the decision for Susan to sleep in the closet after her night shift while I stayed with the kids until around noon, when I would have to wake Susan up from a sound sleep so I could go out and start "cold-calling". Our hope was that by sleeping in the closet, Susan could cop a few hours of sleep.

That same closet would later become our third child's bedroom. You see, we only had a three-bedroom house. Our two older kids each had their own room, and then we had Anthony. Also, since Anthony was just a baby, Susan wanted to be near him while he slept, so we got Susan out of the closet and Anthony into it. But there was now the problem that the closet didn't have a window or any way to get a little ventilation.

We agreed to spend money we didn't have to do something that seemed a tad unusual. We asked a local neighborhood contractor, a laid-back, hard-working guy by the name of Dickie, to cut a small window in the closet so Susan could crack the window and let in some fresh air. Dickie was country-talkin' and down-to-earth, and one of the nicest guys you'd ever meet. He could fix just about anything. Like us, he was a dog lover. And yes, just like Henry Stone and Mr. Moore, at first glance Dickie came off as a little gruff. Once you got past that, he would give you the shirt off his back. He could have charged more for his services, but he didn't care about money. He didn't try to gouge you, and since I wasn't great at fixing things, he was able to help us with a lot of repairs around the house. He was a godsend, especially during a time when we were broke. I remember when we first started talking to him about how to get more air into Susan's soundproof closet.

"Hey, Dickie, we need a small window right here," I said, pointing to the outside wall of the closet. "Can you cut through these bricks to make a window?"

In the way only Dickie could respond, he said with a slight smirk and a goofy grin, "You sure you wanna do that?"

"Yeah, I'm sure," I said. "Susan isn't happy with it, and wants a window so Anthony can sleep in the closet and get some fresh air."

"If mamma ain't happy, nobody's happy," Dickie said, realizing the importance of getting the window into the closet. "When do you want 'er done?"

Dickie went on to cut through those bricks and install a beautiful window for Susan. That man could build anything. Another time, we had some shelves we needed built. He constructed them ahead of time and brought them into our home. To our great surprise and delight, they fit perfectly. For people who take pride in their work and want to help others, it's not always about the money. Dickie genuinely loved what he did. He continued working because he enjoyed helping others. Like Larry preaching at the radio station, it wasn't about the twenty-dollar bill. It was about getting his message out to radio listeners, and expressing his love for the gospel. Dickie expressed himself through handiwork and these finished projects.

I still talk to Dickie, by the way. He's semi-retired now, but only because it's hard for him to work at this stage of life. His funny, no-nonsense approach to life and work, his cynicism—it is all still pretty right-on. I've noticed a common trait shared by hardworking people: most are pretty no-nonsense. Like Dickie, they can see the BS in people pretty quickly. As I get older, I'm finding myself agreeing more and more with their matter-of-fact attitudes about life, money, and people.

Dickie was, in many ways, a great support system for Susan and me during our most difficult years, and I'm grateful to him for that.

As you can see, much of my lifelong success was due to my wife's unwavering support—and the concept of We Money. Everyone needs a support system to accomplish their goals, whether it's to build a shelf or keep the money coming in as you're starting a business. I truly believed then as I do now that no man is an island. Thankfully, We Money is still an important concept for us. Although I'm still working without wondering when I'll retire, we still spend our We Money based on the foundation of mutual respect we built together.

This mutual respect of We Money means supporting each other even if the purchase seems stupid. Take, for example, the possum story. Back in time when our kids were playing youth sports, I did a lot of coaching. Once, while driving by a neighbors house, I spotted a huge 70 foot long batting cage equipped with full netting and a pitching machine to throw baseballs for batting practice. I stopped and asked the owner if he would sell it to me. He did - the whole package for $2,000. At the time, I thought it was a steal! I had to have these big poles hauled over to my home. I was so proud of the batting cage and thought about it as I was driving to work. Susan called me later and said in a mock-sarcastic voice, "Well, your batting cage is working really well." I knew immediately that something was wrong. "Why?" I asked. "Well, there's a possum tangled up in the netting of YOUR batting cage and it can't get out." This was how Susan reacted to yet another of my harebrained schemes. She had a good attitude about everything, even when I had to sell the batting cage years later for a mere $300 just to have it taken away.

Looking back, I still thank God for Susan. Back in those early days of our marriage, her hard work and steady earnings kept us afloat. Today she works part-time in an oncology treatment room. She doesn't work because she has to, but because she wants to.

The bottom line of We Money is that husbands and wives need to make it about them and not allow money to control the unity of their marriage. With our mutual respect for each other in money and love, Susan and I have had a happy marriage. As we face traditional retirement age, Susan has been able to work a reduced schedule, thanks to my business doing well. Many people ask me whether I'll be next to retire, especially since that's my business. For more and more people, this is becoming a harder question to answer, and we'll tackle it in the next chapter against the backdrop of one of my beloved hobbies: playing golf.

Live Well, Die Broke Takeaway #3:
Don't let money come between you and your relationship.

Are you married or getting married soon? Have you ever thought about the concept of We Money? A successful marriage depends on We Money. And the Live Well, Die Broke philosophy encourages couples to think of We Money as *our* money. Life's too short to fight over money. Get on the same page and respect each other's wants and desires. To do so will create a level of mutual respect when it comes to your money and your future together.

Chapter 4

You Can Only Play So Much Golf

Throughout my life, I've never thought about retirement for myself. I never intended to slow down in my career and business. Today, I'm known by my peers in this industry as someone who has always been on the cutting edge of helping Savers worry less about money. I have produced a lot of business and am one of the leading writers of annuities in the country. For more than three decades, I've been on television, sharing with Savers how to better use, enjoy, and protect their money in retirement. I've written five books (this is my sixth). I continue to meet with at least thirty people face-to-face per week. I guess you could say I truly have my finger on the pulse of what Savers are looking to do with their money and their lives.

As long as I continue to enjoy my work and make a decent living doing it, I'll continue to do it for as long as I can. Throughout all of the experiences with my family, I've considered a day when I will need to slow down, but never really thought about full-blown retirement for myself.

Not Granddad. He stopped working as soon as he was fully vested in his employer-provided pension plan. His loyalty to BellSouth over a forty-three-year period bore the fruit of his Mailbox Money. My dad? He never retired. Unfortunately, at the young age of fifty-eight, he was diagnosed with Alzheimer's disease and died in a nursing home just a few years after the diagnosis. Another life lesson for yours truly is that you never know what life might throw your way, so you need to enjoy the days while you still can.

Two generations of family behind me, and now one in front of me, started to make me wonder where I stood with retirement. I started to hear people talk about slowing down or quitting completely. I was even tempted to spend more time away from the office nurturing my favorite hobby, otherwise known as the poster child of a traditional retirement: golf.

For me, golf is not so much about the score, although that's important, but more about the escape from my day-to-day work life. To prove my love and passion for golf, this past year I took a few days off from work and traveled out to Carmel Valley in Monterey, California, for an event called Extraordinary Golf. For three days, I and four other students/golfers (one came all the way from Iceland—yes, you can golf in Iceland) pounded hundreds of golf balls as the two coaches watched and helped us think through our game. This was more than a quick nine on the course; we were being immersed in the sport by some of the best, with a unique philosophy of constantly asking why we were playing and how we could make the game of golf more fun and extraordinary. My background and interest in psychology ate this stuff up.

After a full three days of instruction, the two instructors held a debriefing of the event with the five of us. They wanted to know what we had learned. After the other four students had shared their take on the school, it was my turn. The instructors turned to me, anxious to hear what I'd learned. I said, "I learned this is about as good as I'm going to get at golf." They were shocked at my response. But to me this made complete sense. I had attended the school to see what it might take to get even better, and what I'd learned is that for me golf is not about the score but about the experience. The experience of enjoying the course, the ability to walk (yes, I love walking the course—it's a lot more fun than riding around in a cart), hitting a great shot, just being out there. As the late, great evangelist Billy Graham used to say about golf, "Being on the golf course is the closest thing to heaven on earth."

Speaking of golf, one of my favorite people is the late Buddy Demling. Buddy, a well-known professional golfer in the state of Kentucky, was a former pro and trick-shot artist. Buddy was a rare breed. I met Buddy and his late wife, Sarah, some ten years ago. They showed up to one of my financial workshops and became clients soon thereafter. After getting to know them both, and playing a few rounds of golf with Buddy, I found in this man a person who truly enjoyed life (and golf). When his wife Sarah predeceased Buddy, he called me shortly after her death and said, "Tony, I'm selling our home and moving into a two-bedroom apartment. I need to invest some money and keep it safe. I just want to finish out this life playing golf and spending time with my grandson. Sound good to you?"

Regarding the game of golf, Buddy once told me three things about golf and how to enjoy it for the rest of your life. First, he always said, as you get older, move up to the next tee box. For those of you not familiar with golf, the courses have different tee boxes from which to hit. The course where I play has five per hole with each tee box about 25 to 50 yards closer to the hole. The idea is that for those that don't hit as far, i.e., the older golfers like me, you are allowed to "move up" to the next tee box so that you can get a better shot at making par. As Buddy used to say, there's five tee boxes on each hole for a reason. Don't let your ego get in the way of having a good time. "Move up!" he'd say. His thought about golf was to try to shoot par. In other words, why set yourself up for failure by hitting from tee boxes that are out of your range. So golf rule number one: Move up!

Golf rule number 2: Whatever you do, always try to keep the ball in the fairway. Hit it in the fairway, Buddy would say, and you'll always have a better chance at making par. Hit the ball in the rough, and you won't.

Finally, he'd always say, particularly when I'd quiz him about various ways to swing a club and a lot of that other goofy stuff that tends to mess with your mind and create confusion, "Quit making this game so darn complicated . . . keep it simple." You see, what I've learned about golf and life. Each and every day, we all get to step up on the tee box of life. The question is, what is our approach to the game? To help us think this through, I put together this chart to show how golf and life are very much alike.

	Golf	Live Well, Die Broke
Move up	☑	☑
Keep it in the fairway	☑	☑
Keep it simple	☑	☑

The point is that in my thirty-five years of watching folks try to manage their money, I've discovered that Buddy's three lessons on enjoying golf pertain to both money and life. Like life, golf is what you make of it. You get to decide your approach to the game. To me, golf is an escape. It's also about exercise and spending time meditating on the joys of life, the beauty of the course, and, yes, sometimes an extraordinary golf shot. Golf also includes a nice piece of beautifully manicured land, which is getting harder to find. The golf course is the place where I can leave my work behind and just be present in the moment of an extraordinary activity that I truly enjoy. What's not to like about that?

I'm sure people are thinking, "Haven't you worked hard enough? Don't you have enough to retire?" To which I'd say, yeah, I could retire now and play a bunch of golf but, for me, "You can only play so much golf." Golf is my escape, but it's not a way of life. Golf is a big part of my life, but it is not my life. My life's work is doing what I'm doing right now, which is trying to share what little wisdom and knowledge I have gained over the years. My mission in life is to do what I can to share what I've learned about money and life. My desire is to encourage others to gain this liberating perspective of living well and dying broke.

While some might spend their retirement golf-ing 24/7, which is fine by me and something Buddy certainly enjoyed doing, yes, seven days a week, the vision of retirement as golfing full-time wasn't for me.

I keep it as a respite from the rest of my life and bring back all of the passion and ideas I get on the grass. If you can go out and play on a manicured lawn with no worries and have these extraordinary moments, why wouldn't you?

This is what I call redefining retirement, which I've watched in my own family as the generations have passed. Granddad saw retirement as Mailbox Money, a consistent reward for a lifetime of a job well done. My dad lived in the moment as a musician traveling and playing at the country clubs when he wasn't toiling as a low-paid social worker. For me, retirement is taking extended periods on the golf course and returning to the office with new ideas.

Like Billy Graham, golf is a spiritual practice for me. After a hard day's work, I look forward to life just being me and the ball. I look for those extraordinary shots on the course. I seek out those extraordinary moments that might take my breath away. Often, there are two or three shots that are awesome and that make the afternoon worthwhile. It's like life: if you'll just stay on the course and keep swinging, good things will eventually happen. As a bonus, I'll clear my head enough that I get inspiration about my business. When your mind clears, it focuses your perspective on how thankful you are to do what you do. In that sense, practicing gratitude on the golf course means I'm recharging and ready to hit the ground running on Monday morning.

Let me tell you about a couple I counseled in my office. This husband and wife were ready for retirement, and seemed to be on the glide path for a golf-filled traditional one. But a desire within each of them began to build. They looked at each other and then began telling me about their dreams. They wanted to start a nonprofit organization whose sole purpose would be to provide medical missionary work to third-world countries. This was something they had wanted to do together for years. The only trouble, or at least the trouble as they originally thought, was that they were going to have to dip into their retirement savings to pull it off. A definite test of faith.

Two years later, they are very active and excited about the 501(c)(3) organization they have created. They are traveling the world and helping tons of kids with medical issues that otherwise would go undetected in their poverty-stricken countries. They have purpose and passion. Problem is, as they stated in a follow-up meeting where we reviewed their finances, they were spending more of their retirement money than they had originally planned. I asked them how they felt about that. While they admitted to feeling a tad fearful over the future, they really felt like this was where God had put them and that they needed to do this mission work while they could.

Much to their surprise, I agreed. Now, don't get me wrong, we had to review and make some slight changes, but the purpose of that meeting allowed them to gain confidence that their money was being spent the way God was leading them, like the Soul Sister Trio and Pastor Larry plonking down twenty dollars each week some forty years ago to share the gospel on the radio.

You see, this couple was operating on We Money, and both had the same goals with it. They were doing what they always wanted, which was more important than having a stack of money languishing in their 401(k) or anything else they could be doing. Their retirement, as all potential and current retirees should start thinking about, is not all about sitting on a pile of money. It's truly about finding purpose. After all, life is short, which I see examples of in my office constantly. I met a fifty-six-year-old man who had a serious operation on his blood vessels. I've also had clients pass away as they were about to retire, never to get the chance to use and enjoy the fruits of their labor. Seeing those regrets and what-ifs is what keeps me counseling people in my business.

This is also where the Guilt-Trip Gospel, which you've been seeing throughout the book, comes in heavily. These individuals are ready to retire and enjoy their money, but feel guilty for doing what they want. Maybe they don't want to play golf forever, but there's pressure on them to do retirement in that way.

Or there's the other side, which has some of them feeling weird about being retired when their friends are still working. You retire because you've done a good job of saving for retirement, and many of your friends may still have to work because they have not. I see it all the time: the ones who have planned feel guilty because they can retire and their friends cannot. It's another example of the Guilt-Trip Gospel playing havoc with your ability to enjoy the journey.

Why does this happen? For many people who are still working and can't retire, it's not a matter of still having to work; it's that they haven't made a plan for how they could live well and die broke. For example, I've witnessed high-income earners who would like to retire, but can't afford to because they have overspent and undersaved. You'd think on the surface that some-one who's making big bucks could easily retire with the salary they make. However, they often get in their own way, and this leads to them not retiring and put-ting other people on the Guilt-Trip Gospel. Worse still, these individuals may feel entitled in not ever retir-ing, leading to a never-ending cycle where they both bemoan and celebrate never retiring, and in essence never getting to do the things they've always wanted to do. That trip or goal in life will always be out of reach, as long as they talk about not retiring with those who are ready to retire and are planning to do so.

People's excitement about retiring can be tempered by these feelings. When I talked with the missionary-to-be couple, I encouraged them to pursue their defi-nition of retirement. I wanted them to feel empowered by their choices and make their own decisions. Most importantly, I wanted them to be happy with those decisions for the long-term future. I told them not to worry about what other people thought about their plans, and I could see on their faces a mixture of relief and anticipation about the next step in their lives.

In the next chapter, I'll show you how the Guilt-Trip Gospel traveled through generations of my family, and how you can stop it in yours for good.

Live Well, Die Broke Takeaway #4:
Redefine your definition of retirement.

What's your vision for retirement, and what are other important things in your life besides retirement? What is it you truly enjoy doing? Look for the little things in life that don't cost any money (walking on a golf course versus riding in a cart). If life's getting a little harder, move up to a tee box that puts you in a better and more enjoyable position. I never plan on retiring, but I know I'll have to slow down some day—in other words, I'll have to move up to the next tee box. Don't make it so hard on yourself. Do the things you love doing for as long as possible, but make it easier along the way. See what I mean?

```
1072
   RN
(AP)-KENTUCKY SPOT NEWS

   (SINKING CHURCH)
   (FRANKLIN) -- MEMBERS OF A WESTERN KENTUCKY CHURCH THAT IS
COLLAPSING INTO A SINK HOLE ARE TRYING TO SAVE AT LEAST PART OF THE
BUILDING. THE DRAKESBORO METHODIST CHURCH HAS 19 STAINED GLASS WINDOWS
-- EACH MEASURING FROM FOUR TO EIGHT FEET LONG -- THAT DATE BACK TO
1919.
   MEMBERS WANT TO RECOVER THE PRICELESS WINDOWS IN CASE THE BUILDING
IS SWALLOWED INTO THE HOLE. BUT TODAY -- THEY LEARNED FROM AN ENGINEER
THAT REMOVING THE WINDOWS COULD CAUSE THE STRUCTURE'S IMMEDIATE
COLLAPSE. ANOTHER ENGINEER FROM PENNSYLVANIA ARRIVED IN DRAKESBORO
TONIGHT TO STUDY THE PROBLEM FURTHER.
   ------(DASH)------
   FIRE CHIEF ROBERT STOVER SAYS THE SINKHOLE -- WHICH IS LOCATED ABOVE
AN UNDERGROUND MINE -- MEASURED 50 OR 75 FEET IN DIAMETER TODAY. HE
SAYS CRACKS DEVELOPED IN THE WALLS OF THE CHURCH WHEN THE LAND AROUND
THE BUILDING BEGAN SINKING YESTERDAY.
   (TONY WALKER, WFKN)

AP-LX-10-07-82 2048EDT
```

1982 - Tony's first AP news story hits the wire while working at WFKN radio as a part-time reporter

1932 - Tony's grandfather upper left at the age of 18. To his left, his granddad along with two of granddad's brothers

**Tony's father and mother's "dance band"
in 1960. Upper left, Tony's Dad,
to his left, Tony's Mom. Lower left,
drummer, Johnnie Higgins and lower far
right, bass player, Bill Farris**

Tony's granddad, far upper left-hand corner, in 1951 in an engineering meeting in Louisville Kentucky with other Bell South engineers

Christmas at Granddad's house. Pretty simple huh. That's uncle Eddie on the left, Granddad standing and his beloved wife, Hazel

1984 - Tony ditches his dream of being the next Tom Brokaw and begins his financial services career with his father-in-law, Bill Moore

DISABILITY AND SERVICE RETIREMENTS WITH SURVIVOR OPTION   FORM 8544-6 (6-79)

South Central Bell

P. O. BOX 771
BIRMINGHAM, ALA. 35201
(205) 321-3540 OR 3542

APRIL 14, 1980

HARDIN/WILLIAM E

DEAR RETIREE:

WE PREVIOUSLY ANNOUNCED A SPECIAL 16 PER CENT PER MONTH INCREASE OF YOUR PRESENT PENSION FOR THOSE WHO RETIRED BEFORE THE END OF JANUARY, 1977. FOR THOSE WHO RETIRED AFTER JANUARY, 1977, THE INCREASE IS APPROXIMATELY .45 PER CENT PER MONTH FOR EACH FULL OR PARTIAL MONTH OF RETIREMENT FROM THE EFFECTIVE DATE OF THE PENSION THROUGH NOVEMBER, 1979.

YOUR NEW PENSION AMOUNT IS SHOWN BELOW AND DOES NOT INCLUDE ANY MEDICARE REIMBURSEMENT YOU MAY BE RECEIVING IN YOUR PENSION CHECK. THE FIRST PAYMENT OF THIS INCREASE WILL BE INCLUDED IN YOUR PENSION CHECK FOR THE MONTH OF APRIL, 1980 TO BE RECEIVED ABOUT MAY 1, 1980.

SINCE THE INCREASE WAS AUTHORIZED TO BE EFFECTIVE DECEMBER 1, 1979, YOUR CHECK FOR THE MONTH OF APRIL WILL ALSO INCLUDE THE MAKE-UP PAYMENT FOR THE FOUR-MONTH PERIOD FROM DECEMBER, 1979 THROUGH MARCH, 1980.

SINCE YOU HAD ELECTED THE SURVIVOR OPTION WHEN YOU RETIRED, YOUR ANNUITANT'S PENSION, WHEN PAYABLE, WILL BE INCREASED BY THE SAME PERCENTAGE, AS WAS APPLIED TO YOUR PENSION.

EFFECTIVE DECEMBER 1, 1979
_____

MONTHLY AMOUNT OF SPECIAL INCREASE $42.70

TOTAL NEW MONTHLY PENSION AMOUNT $665.03, LESS PRESENT DEDUCTIONS

FOR ANNUITANT WHEN PAYABLE $332.52

SINCERELY,

C. B. MEHAFFEY, SECRETARY
EMPLOYEES' BENEFIT COMMITTEE

Evidence of Granddad's beloved Mailbox Money he and Hazel would receive for the rest of their lives.

Tony (on the left) and his brother Marty, sitting in Granddad's little barn in Troy, Kentucky.

1956 - Tony's dad on a weekend home from college, standing with his mom outside the little store his father ran in Drakesboro, Kentucky

JAN 1956

Tony's mom (far left), along with Granny Walker and one of her daughters, shortly after his mom married Dad. This was her first visit to the big city of Drakesboro, Kentucky.

1983 - Tony and his new bride, Susan, shortly after she received her B.S. in nursing

Tony at the home of granddad in Troy, Kentucky, shortly after his retirement from Bell South in 1978.

1963 - The front porch of Tony's home as a kid in Lexington. Brother Marty, (far left), Tony in the middle and Dad. Today, Tony's mom still lives in the same home

WBRC-TV
ATOP RED MOUNTAIN·BOX 6 BIRMINGHAM, AL. 35201

July 18, 1983

Tony Walker
1310 ½ Euclid Ave.
Bowling Green, Kentucky 42101

Dear Mr. Walker:

Thank you for your interest in WBRC-TV. I've reviewed your
application for a position in sports, but at this point am
unable to offer you employment.

We will keep your application on file.

Sincerely,

Brian Bracco
News Director

BB/bs

Tony's first of many response letters from various TV stations, suggesting Tony consider another line of work

Tony's beloved 1962 VW Beetle, gifted to him by his granddad, along with his high-school sweetheart, Susan, in 1976

Chapter 5

LETTING GO OF THE GUILT-TRIP GOSPEL FOR GOOD

It was around the age of 50 that my dad finally started planning for retirement. I remember him coming home one day saying that a guy at work said he should start putting aside in his 403(b) plan at work...which Dad quickly began. He never thought of it himself, and continued to be a social worker by day and a musician by night. As I mentioned earlier, due to a sudden turn for the worse in his health and his death at the age of sixty-four, Dad never ended up retiring. On the other hand, my father-in-law didn't need anyone to tell him to plan for his future. He was way ahead of that game. For years, not only had he been saving and building his business, but he also understood the potential value of real estate, buying and selling condos. People who knew him or knew of him sometimes resented the fact that during his working years, he was able to take so much time off from work. True to his plans, Mr. Moore was able to walk away from the business at a time in his life when he could still travel and spend the winters down at his condominium in Fort Myers, Florida. He was a true planner and his plans usually worked out.

For some strange reason, people often get ridiculed for their success, but success isn't defined by millions of dollars, even in retirement. There are a lot of people I meet who think that they have to have millions of dollars to retire on. They've bought into the narrative promoted by Wall Street and the big 401(k) companies that you probably won't have enough money in retirement, so don't retire or, when you do, be careful about spending it. These big institutions have a huge conflict of interest in offering such goofy advice, since they don't want you to retire and enjoy your money because that means you'll be taking it from them. Understand that it is hard for them to make money on our money if we're taking it from them and spending it.

Most people I meet do have enough money to retire, or at least slow down. And yes, sometimes that retirement might look a tad different than they'd envisioned, but nevertheless they can make it with some help and guidance. Believe it or not, I've seen people with very little who are able to retire, while I've seen people with lots of money who cannot. It all comes down to cash flow—money coming in versus money going out. It is up to each of us to decide how that cash flow will play out.

Although people are retiring in a very different economy than Granddad, they can still follow the concepts of Mailbox Money, adhering to We Money in their relationships, and redefining their own retirement. I've taken these concepts and incorporated them into my own life. One of the biggest issues of current generations (millennials and Gen Yers) is not *when* they will retire but *if* they will retire. My children are millennial-aged and are facing these issues. As we'll explore further in Chapter 7, no one is helping them make sound financial decisions. Instead, they are encouraged to get into more student loan debt, while unable to afford basic living arrangements. With the average student loan debt of $28,650 and more young adults living at home, there's the newfound likelihood that, as a result, they and their parents will have less money in the future to retire on.

In reaction to this changing economy, millennials are changing jobs instead of staying in them. Many jobs no longer have a pension as a carrot for retirement. Instead, they are being replaced by 401(k)s, which if invested in the stock market can be very volatile and unpredictable. With that said, studies reveal that millennials don't see the point in contributing to them. In an ironic callback to past money stories, my millenial aged children have little interest in risking their money in the stock market. However, while Granddad enjoyed his employer-sponsored pension plan as his mailbox money - they won't. It truly is a dilemma for this age group.

Sandwiched between my dad's and my children's generations, and with an eye toward Granddad's generation, I've gotten on the Guilt-Trip Gospel about how I'm spending my own money. Since I'm worried about the next generation not having any money, I give a lot of money to my grown kids. When I die, I plan to leave them some tax-free money, but I also want to watch them use and enjoy some of my money while I'm alive. My concerns over their financial future has led me to want to assist them both while I'm alive and when I'm dead and gone.

I've gotten off the Guilt-Trip Gospel about giving my children money. I'm also allowing myself to see the world as it is now, not the way it was or the way it will be in thirty years' time. Today is a different world from the one in which Granddad shook hands with a Bell-South manager and got a job. It's different from when Dad talked his way into a college bowling instructor job. It's even different from when I shook hands with Mr. Moore and started getting insurance experience that I'd take into my own business. Today's generation has more logistical hoops to jump through for everything they want to do. Why not make it easier for the ones you love? At least, that's how I want to live well and die broke. What will the economy look like in twenty or thirty years from now? I'm not worried about it.

Hopefully my children won't either, thanks to how I'm using and enjoying my money now.

Speaking of leaving money behind, the next chapter is all about how being on the receiving end of inheritance is not necessarily a ticket to paradise.

Live Well, Die Broke Takeaway #5:
Don't feel guilty doing with your money what others feel you shouldn't.

While some people might think giving your grown children money now is unusual, I would challenge that well-worn assumption and say that leaving your children money after you're gone is more absurd. It's important to live in the moment and provide for loved ones because that's what you truly want to do, as long as that's what you're getting off the Guilt-Trip Gospel is about.

Chapter 6

GET OFF THAT WALLET, DEE-DEE!

Susan got the news over the phone that her mother, Dee-Dee, had passed away from cancer. It was expected, but still sad for Susan and her family. My mother-in-law, whom I'd first met when I was sixteen years old, had successfully battled lung cancer some eight years before, only to see it come raging back and take her life in just a few short weeks.

Of course, Susan was devastated. She had just lost her best friend, and now her mother. After going through the planning of a funeral and the service itself, there was one more formality: Dee-Dee's attorney providing Susan with a copy of her mother's will. Much to Susan's surprise, she would be receiving an inheritance.

Like so many people I counsel who have received inheritances, this was not a joyful experience . In fact, what I've discovered about inheritance is that sometimes it can be more of a curse than a blessing.

You see, when it comes to losing a loved one and getting money, the beneficiary (recipient) of that money, is likely to experience a certain amount of guilt. This is a specific kind of guilt, which is different from the Guilt-Trip Gospel. My wife didn't want the money—she wanted her mother back, and no amount of money could make that happen.

Even today, some two years after Dee-Dee's passing, my wife continues to struggle with her inheritance and how best to use and enjoy it. I do as well. As I see it, this money is not We Money; it's Susan's money. And while advising people on what to do with inheritances is a daily part of my work as a retirement planning specialist, advising my wife about this particular pot of money is quite awkward. In other words, it was a heck of a lot easier telling Dee-Dee to spend and enjoy her money while she was alive than giving my wife advise on how to handle Dee-Dee's money after she died. Moral to the story: having more money doesn't always mean you'll worry less about it.

Dee-Dee had been a teacher and her husband, Mr. Moore, was the one in charge of the finances. When he passed away, Dee-Dee was left with plenty of money to live on, yet was always anxious about spending it. In fact, she often asked Susan and I what we thought about her future purchases—as if she needed our permission to buy what she was contemplating.

Me? I too just want my mother-in-law back. I just want to go back to the days of me trying to encourage Dee-Dee, while she was very much alive and healthy, to quit hanging on to this money and to try spending and enjoying it. I remember knowing that Dee-Dee had quite a bit of money in her checking account and her asking me if she should purchase a new TV. I replied, "Dee-Dee, you've got plenty of money, now get off that wallet and go get you a TV."

This lesson of a generation coming and a generation going is part of my everyday conversation with clients. I must constantly remind them that life is short and things will change and, of course, you and I will one day die. We will die broke, and all the money in the world won't change that fact. So how about you? Do you need to get off your wallet? My guess is that you do.

Whether you are reading this as the person who is thinking of leaving an inheritance or you're the reader who is or will soon be receiving one, for Susan and many other people inheritance can create a worry that didn't exist before. This is especially true for our generation... as many of us begin to become the first generation of potentially significant inheritances, money our parents have that will soon be ours to deal with. This is very different from our parents, who for the most part didn't receive much of an inheritance from their parents. My mom got a small, dilapidated home in Troy, Kentucky. We will be leaving our kids much, much more.

The recent experience with Susan and Dee-Dee reminds me that while we all need to save for retirement, we have to be careful about stockpiling too much money and not spending any of it. Not only was I seeing this in my own family, but with my clients. One client wanted me to assist her in planning to pay for her grandchildren's private schooling. My financial analysis of her present situation and her current assets helped her to see that she could help her family now, without the fear of running out of money later.

To help you think through this notion of how and when to get off your wallet, I created the Live Well, Die Broke Financial Timeline.

Tony's Live Well, Die Broke Timeline

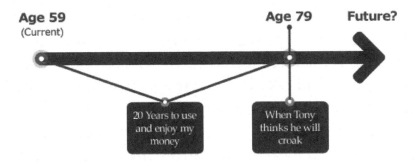

Notice that I'm fifty-nine, soon to be sixty years of age. As you can see, I wrote down the age of 79. What is significant about that age? I know this is going to sound strange, but seventy-nine is the age I think I'll be when I die. Crazy, I agree, and it's not that I know for sure I'll be dead and gone by seventy-nine. The point is when I plot it on this little timeline, something happens to my perspective. I begin to realize that if I knew for sure that age 79 was it for me, I'd only have twenty years left on planet earth! But that's not really the point because what I've seen in working with thousands of people who are my age and older is that I probably only have about another ten "good" years of living it up left. My experience teaches me that as I watch many of my clients age, they tend to spend less money. Their health worsens, they get tired of traveling, yes, even of golfing. So what's the point? The point is that where you place yourself on this timeline will determine your perspective on the remaining years of your life.

Assuming you have in place Mailbox Money of some sort, that is, a source of guaranteed income you can never outlive, then you've got the game beat. You can live well knowing that you can enjoy your money while you can without the fear of it running out, just like my Granddad.

Living well and dying broke is the secret to a happy, satisfying retirement. My wife, in this example, never thought about money from her parents; now that this money has been left to her, she has the huge weight of what to do with it, even though it's been two years since her mom passed. That's where the Live Well, Die Broke philosophy comes in. Before you leave family and friends a boatload of money (which is okay by me), consider whether you should be using and enjoying more of it now. And yes, this enjoyment might mean spending money for and on the kids and grandkids now versus passing it off to them when you die.

Remember, a dollar is not worth anything until it is converted to cash and used. We all die broke.

Live Well, Die Broke Takeaway #6:
Inheriting money is not a sure bet for your retirement, and does not appreciably add to the enjoyment of your life.

In fact, it can even cause stress in your life. Break this cycle for yourself and your loved ones by rethinking inheritance. Put a different spin on money and leaving a bunch of it when you die. Maybe your loved ones could better use some of your money while you're still alive. By giving them money now vs. later, they can use it when they truly need it, and you can see them enjoy it as opposed to being handed it after you die, when they may not need nor want it. Think about that. Living well and dying broke is said in that order for a reason: enjoyment in retirement, or, if you continue working, enjoyment throughout your life.

Chapter 7

TEACHING FINANCIAL LESSONS TO THE NEXT GENERATION

While Dad never taught me how to manage money, he did ingrain in me the notion of always being myself and doing the things in life that I really wanted to do, using my God-given gifts and talents to the best of my ability. I've tried my darndest to impart this philosophy and way of living to my kids.

When each of my children was born, I had dreams for them. Along with my more sentimental hopes that they'd be healthy and feel love throughout their lives, I wondered how they would view money as they grew up. How would they someday earn and invest their own funds? Would they follow in the footsteps of Granddad, Dad, Mom, or Mr. Moore? Would they be good Savers? Would they even be interested in my credo of living well and dying broke?

One related assumption I had about my children was that they would own their own businesses. Or better yet, I thought, what if I could build this business into something cool and, like my father-in-law who had brought in his son and me and another son-in-law, create a family business? In other words, I had in my mind how all of this would play out for them.

When I think about it, I assumed my children would want to be in business in some way, since that was what I experienced as a young person in the business world. My father-in-law, Mr. Moore, brought me into his company, as you read about in a previous chapter, and gave me the tough love to keep at it. The only person in my business today is my son-in-law; none of my kids are in the business. I made sure my son-in-law worked in the business world before I entertained his coming in. He has an appreciation for life outside the business, which makes it easier for us to work together.

In some ways, I'm fine with my kids not being in business with me. Instead, I want them to have the freedom to do with their lives whatever they want. I had the choice to be working the radio station and then going on to my own talk show and writing six books, and I want them to have the same freedom.

As my children got older and needed less direct financial assistance from me for food, shelter, and the basics, I still wanted to provide for them in my unique way. Most parents in my position, as I've seen in my work, would come into my office and talk about leaving an inheritance to their children. Often, my clients feel the only way to give to their children once they're adults is to leave them money when they've passed on.

But as we've seen in the chapter about Susan receiving an inheritance from her mom Dee-Dee, leaving your children money once you're gone can be more of a burden than a relief. Watching Susan go through the anguish over what to do with the money, coupled with my own desire to give to my kids in my own way, led me to financially aid my children in the Live Well, Die Broke tradition. Instead of having as my main objective in life to leave my kids a bunch of money when I die - which I'd like to do - I focused instead on the joy of watching them enjoy my money while I'm still here. It's fun to see how they react and use this money. To me, this process of giving now vs. later makes complete sense.

The truth is, we as parents and grandparents may have stockpiled money that our children and grandchildren can put to work *now*. Millennials have many additional financial challenges than their parents did. My wife and I had very few expenses to deal with at that age. In the 1980s we had no student debt, no technological gadgets and gizmos to pay for, and the cost of housing was much lower than today. In addition, young people have over $1.7 trillion in student debt, and more of them are living at home for much longer with their parents. What can those of us who have money—healthy 401(k)s with plenty of money in them—do for our kids?

The answer is to help them now, while you can. You can even utilize tax laws to give this money as large gifts, tax-free and useful for them, and takes the worry away from you later. Take for example the problem of this country's student debt, which as of the date of this book is estimated to be over $1.7 trillion. Let's imagine your child or grandchild has racked up $50,000 in student debt. Let's say that the interest rate they are paying is 8 percent, and the balance won't be paid off for thirty years (this could be any kind of debt, including credit-card debt). If you take the total cost of those payments, the debt costs them over $100,000—money that is gone forever. But the fun's not over just yet, because the debt is just starting. You see, that $100,000 could have been invested into something that possibly earned interest at 8 percent, which means if there was no student debt, or the funds were provided by you to pay the debt off early, the loss in wealth over their lifetime could exceed one million dollars!

This scenario isn't even about the wealth of one person, who may be your grandchild, losing out on a lifetime of increased income. If they're not able to buy that house or better their life in other ways with additional income, they may put off having children or doing the things they want to do in life. Perhaps your grandson would like to have children one day, but because he can barely afford to pay off his student loans, he postpones those plans indefinitely. This loss of generational wealth could have been prevented if you as the grandparent had considered your retirement fund in a new way and stopped stockpiling money.

In this spirit of giving your children and grandchildren their own financial freedom, I provide for my three children in different ways. I help them buy houses so they and their children don't have to worry about their living situations. This allows them to focus on their passions. My children's burgeoning personalities make an appearance in my office. Behind my desk, there's a picture of my oldest boy Phillip pushing a lawn mower, Lacey washing a car, and Anthony holding out his hand. Each of them developed their own views on money, and it is captured in this one photo.

While all three of my children are hardworking adults, as a kid I'd say that my oldest child, Phillip, had a similar work ethic to me as a young person, working at Wendy's at age sixteen and moving up from cashier to manager. Today, Phillip is a successful nurse practitioner who sees a lot of patients. At thirty-three, he's following in the footsteps of my dad, who worked as a social worker, although he makes more money because he has an advanced degree in what he's doing. Lacey, our second child, was a little less focused on school and work, yet, like me, she always enjoyed talking to others and selling them on her ideas. Of my three children, she is probably the most like me in terms of her personality and her "way with words." She also believes in herself and knows when she's right; as they say, she won't take no for an answer. And she's always been like this, as I'll show you in the following story.

Several years ago while in college, Lacey asked me to book a hotel room in Florida for spring break for her and a few friends. She sent me the link to the hotel, whose website boasted nice rooms and a beautiful pool and view of the ocean. I paid for the room and hoped they would all have a good time on their break from school. Off they went to Florida. The start of their vacation turned out very differently than the website had led them to believe it would, however. They saw, as they were pulling into the parking lot of this hotel, that the place was a dump; there were cop cars everywhere, as there had apparently just been an incident there. As the girls proceeded to check into their rooms, they noticed that the hotel looked nothing like the pictures posted on the site. It clearly was a dump!

In true Lacey fashion, she immediately complained to the manager and asked for their deposit back, as they were going to go elsewhere. The hotel manager would have none of that, and basically told them that if they didn't stay, they would lose all of their deposit. Lacey called me in tears, feeling awful that they would lose the deposit I'd put down for them. Being over a thousand miles away and not knowing what to tell her, I told her it was fine and to just find another place.

Little did I know that Lacey had confronted the manager. Remember, she was only nineteen years old at the time. She sat in the lobby of the locally owned hotel and waited for the owner to show up. When the owner arrived, Lacey introduced herself, but he walked past her as if she wasn't there. Big mistake on his part. As he was proceeding to his office, Lacey walked right behind him and into the office to demand a refund of their deposit. He refused. Lacey would later tell me, in that moment, she noticed a picture of him and a young lady. She pointed to the picture and asked the owner, "May I ask who that is?" He said, "That's me and my daughter." Knowing she had him where she wanted him, Lacey said, "Would you want your daughter staying here?" And the guy didn't say anything. He seemed stunned, and clearly Lacey had found his Achilles' heel. This man would never let his daughter stay in a place like that, and he promptly refunded the money.

Lacey has a degree in nursing, runs an online business, and currently chooses to stay home full-time and raise her and her husband's two children. Speaking of my favorite son-in-law and Lacey's husband, Trey, he is doing a great job of working with me in my business. Like her dad, Lacey definitely has the entrepreneurial spirit of the generations in her family. She's very creative and a skilled amateur photographer. Lacey took photos of her toddler daughter, Scout, dressed in scarves; the scarf company saw this photo on Instagram and gave Lacey more scarves. Lacey also shares the photos with the other companies who make the clothing Scout is wearing in different photos. In exchange for the vendors using the photos of Scout on their websites, Lacey receives free clothes and money. Even with her two kids and a very busy life, she's productive and using her entrepreneurial skills. She's the only one who could really go out and do what I've done with my own business. I think she'll continue her entrepreneurial endeavors..

What Lacey's doing is indicative of what's going on with her generation when it comes to generating their own version of Mailbox Money. While there aren't as many opportunities for pensions or what Granddad would consider Mailbox Money, millennials are using social media and the Internet to do this for themselves. This means if you're a stay-at-home mom like Lacey, or you can't afford an office space like Mr. Moore back in the day, and who had to rely on that insurance money to pay the bills, there's another way to do it.

Even though Lacey is home full-time, her part-time online business allows her to receive a monthly check—Mailbox Money—from working from home. This Mailbox Money is just like Granddad's; it's a dependable amount of money that comes in every month. Lacey wants to stay at home and raise her kids, and she can still pursue her entrepreneurial dreams. For example, Lacey loves to work out. When she went into her local gym and noticed there was an opportunity for them to use Instagram more effectively, as she's been doing with Scout's photos, Lacey bartered with them that she would work on their Instagram in exchange for free membership.

Given Lacey's entrepreneurial passion, I in turn can help her pursue this passion. Today's generation of baby boomers has substantial liquid income to work with (assuming their parents are gifting money to them during lifetime or at death). They can get creative and help their kids in ways they didn't think was possible. Instead of building bigger barns, I can help Lacey and her husband Trey own a home that they can enjoy and subsequently we can enjoy with them and their children. Lacey can then afford to stay at home with the kids while freeing her mind to consider other entrepreneurial pursuits she wouldn't have had the time to consider otherwise. Now she can have a baby on her hip and punch into a computer with the other hand, all while not worrying about whether she can afford to be in her home.

My youngest, Anthony, a by-the-book millennial, couldn't care less about accumulating stuff. He doesn't really think about retirement and certainly has no desire to risk his money by investing it in the stock market. Anthony's also one of the most contented and simple young adults you'll ever meet. He, just like Phillip and Lacey, is a hard worker and currently has an interest in the movie-theatre business, and currently works as an assistant manager at a local movie house. Will he ever come into my business? I doubt it, but that's okay by me. As long as he is happy and healthy, I'm good with that.

By the way, I know my generation tends to think that millennials don't want to work; my thoughts are that they do, they just work differently than we do. Gone is the notion of working nine-to-five. They want to work when *they* want to work. This bunch grew up with computers and technology. They know they can get just as much done sitting at home in their boxer shorts at 3 a.m. as taking the time to come into an office all dressed up and grind it out for an eight-hour stretch.

These are new opportunities millennials are taking advantage of, and their baby-boomer parents should take note. This generation is creating their own version of Mailbox Money, and they're taking full advantage of it. In addition, my children are carrying along the money stories of my family into the future. Remember that example about the grandma helping her grandson pay off his student loan debt and allowing him to use that money to further his life goals? Imagine what millennials will do with their own money when their children are old enough. Imagine how they can contribute to the long line of generational wealth in their own families simply by being more present and not holding on to money their children can enjoy now.

In fact, millennials actually know better than any other generation that holding on to a stockpile of money does more harm than good. As mentioned earlier, baby boomers are the first generation to begin receiving substantial inheritances from their parents. Today, millennials can recognize the burden of inheritance as Susan experienced, and they are paving their own roads for future generations to live well and die broke.

To that end, I'm happy to help my children while Susan and I are still here. As I mentioned in a previous chapter, I will go on to provide financial assistance for my grown children while I am alive. I want to watch them flourish and not worry about what happens with the economy. This gives me greater peace than knowing I will leave them money after I am gone. I can watch them enjoy and make a difference with the money now.

Live Well, Die Broke Takeaway #7:
Don't assume your kids will handle money the way you do.

Don't try and convince them to use, spend, or save money as you do. If they aren't as interested in something or don't enjoy what they're doing, encourage them to find something else to do. If they have an interest in something, even if you don't, encourage them to be the best they can be in the pursuit of that interest and give it all they've got. In my practice of meeting with hundreds upon hundreds of people, I've run into a lot of parents who take the blame for how their kids are doing both personally and financially. Maybe their kids aren't on the right track or "making something of themselves," whatever that means. Usually a phrase like that has more to do with the parent than the child, and speaks to the parent's discomfort about what their child is doing in the world (and what *they* may not like). Regardless, you can only do so much, and there's no shame in loving and providing for them as best you can. Parenting is tough stuff, and what I'm still discovering is that no two kids (or three, in my case) are exactly alike.

In the end, whether your kid grows up to be a brain surgeon or a fry-cook, who cares! The main thing is that they are happy and healthy and doing their part to have a positive influence on others, no matter how much money they are making or saving in the process. And whether they have children of their own or not, empowering your children through these kinds of financial choices may lead them to help others later on. Perhaps your children will start nonprofits that provide meals to those in need, or will find their niche in the market for their own business. Remember, this is about a new way of thinking: Live Well, Die Broke.

Chapter 8

LIFE IS TOO SHORT TO EAT CHEAP BACON

Even though my mom has very little money, she is one of the most financially content people I've ever known. Since my parents' divorce in 1970, she has never remarried and never complained about her financial situation. I've always admired that about her. She still lives in the same house we grew up in, drives a twenty-plus-year-old car, and spends very little on herself. She is thankful for what she has, and she watches every penny. Mom is very good with money and knows the value of a dollar. I remember Granddad once saying, "Your mother is so tight with money that she wouldn't pay a dime to see an ant eat a bale of hay."

Yet, as content as Mom is with living on very little, one thing she will not skimp on is good bacon. Mom is one of the biggest fans of this breakfast staple; it's the one item she will definitely get off her wallet and purchase.

Growing up in Kentucky, bacon was a necessity in our house. I'm not sure about the rest of the country, but who doesn't like bacon? My mom, who has to live paycheck to paycheck in her senior years, is still one of the biggest fans of this breakfast staple. One of the things she won't cut back on is the quality of her bacon, which I learned about on a visit with her.

Recently, while I stayed over at my mom's house, I awoke to a wonderful breakfast of bacon and eggs. As usual, Mom was very concerned that the bacon she had last purchased was not "very good." As she watched me pick up that lovely, crispy piece of bacon and take my first bite, she anxiously asked, "How's the bacon?" I replied, "Excellent."

She seemed very pleased and then revealed her version of what I would call first class: "I paid $10 for that pound of bacon," she proudly announced.

At first, I was a little surprised Mom would pay that much for bacon, but then I remembered my own advice: whether we have a little or a lot of money, there's always something we want to treat ourselves to. The Live Well, Die Broke philosophy says that if we're sensible with our money most of the time, why not indulge in what we want some of the time—yes, that even includes a $10 pound of bacon.

Indulging in a pleasure or two with the money you have is the ticket to a happier life. In my mom's case, buying a $10 pound of bacon each week is a small price to pay for the enjoyment it brings her and the moment she and I can share over breakfast.

I had a couple come into my office who demonstrate this idea of finding your own version of first class. They were in their seventies and in good health, with a good income and plenty of money to live on. They love to travel to Europe on a regular basis and partake in very expensive river cruises, the ones that only include about 100 guests and provide first-class service to all of their voyagers. The cruises were very expensive. While updating their retirement plan, I asked them if they fly first class to get to these destinations. Their answer was "No. It's too expensive".

"Wait a minute, you're flying coach over ten hours to get to a first-class river cruise?" I said. "That doesn't make sense. What if I said you could afford it?" They looked stunned for a moment, and I said, "I give you permission to fly first class on your next airfare to Europe."

A few months later, this couple came back into my office, smiling and looking refreshed. I asked them how their trip in first class went, and they said, "That was so cool!" They really enjoyed it, and thanked me for convincing them to get off their wallet and go for it. My point is I knew they could afford it, and the experience of flying first class to Europe would mean more enjoyment. This was the perfect example of using your money now and living while you can, and I was thrilled for them. When I can, I also love flying first class and having more legroom and better snacks.

Letting go of the Guilt-Trip Gospel allowed me to avoid getting hung up on every dollar I spent, no matter what I spent it on. Whether it's a 300 dollar round of golf at scenic Spyglass Hill, or six bucks for an overpriced coffee, or $10 for a pound of bacon, we all have our little quirks when it comes to what we spend money on. Guess what? That's okay. It's just money. Don't get all worked up over it and, for goodness' sake, don't put others on a guilt trip for spending money on the things they want.

Letting go of the Guilt-Trip Gospel allowed me to see money for the tool it truly is: a commodity to get what I want and need in life and to help others along the way. There is nothing sacred or spiritual about money. It truly is here today and gone tomorrow. And while I'm all about planning for the future, I'm also all about using and enjoying the fruits of my labor today. That's the balance we all must figure out. Like raising kids, it will be different and look different for all of us. There's no one way "to do money."

In my personal experience, finding my version of "first class" led to my planning a three-day golf trip to Monterey, California to play world-famous Pebble Beach and several other courses. I got off my own wallet and treated my son Anthony, my favorite son-in-law Trey, and my brother Marty to an all-expenses-covered trip from yours truly.

Was it expensive? You bet. Was it memorable? Oh yeah!

In fact, to this day we all talk about how much fun it was to play Pebble Beach. No Guilt-Trip Gospel here.

What's to feel guilty about? We played premier golf courses and ate excellent meals. It has been over two years since we went on that trip, but every time Marty and I play golf, we still talk about how much fun we had together. Not only was it a fantastic time that we still talk about, but it brought me closer to my brother. And isn't getting closer with your friends and family worth the extra money you spend on a once-in-a-life-time vacation?

Whether it's a $10 pound of bacon or forking over more money for first-class tickets (and the better service and snacks it brings), life really is too short to eat cheap bacon. So don't sell yourself short. Now, before we go wild and spend money we don't have, we should follow a simple rule to spending wisely: Don't buy things you don't need in order to impress people you might not like anyway. You still have to be sensible here. To strike a balance between a life of spending and a life of saving, let's take a look at this chapter's Live Well, Die Broke Takeaway.

Live Well, Die Broke Takeaway #8:

Enjoy the simple pleasures of life now, before it's too late.

How about you? What's your $10 pound of bacon story? What is it you're putting off spending on tomorrow that you could easily afford to purchase today? Remember, whether we have a little or a lot, we all die broke. Enjoy the simple pleasures of life now, before it's too late.

Fill in the blank: what's the one thing you would like to do before you die that you haven't done? Write it down now. Then, ask yourself this question: What's keeping you from doing it? What naysaying voice comes up in your head that's telling you to not go for something you enjoy, provided that you're spending sensibly in other parts of your financial life?

Epilogue

GOING . . . GOING . . . GONE

Going . . . going . . . gone. Those final words of the auctioneer as he nailed the coffin on Granddad's last possession,
a modest little home in "the country," are a lesson to all
of us. Gone was Granddad's beloved Mailbox Money.
Gone was his little home. But alive and well were the
fond memories I have and hold to this day.

Fond memories of sitting and relaxing with Granddad and Hazel on their front porch. Memories of
swinging by Long John Silver's Seafood Restaurant for
a modest-size portion of fish and chips. The excitement
I felt when Granddad gave me my first car, his car, a
shiny black Volkswagen Beetle that I absolutely loved.
This was the same little car I drove to take my first high
school sweetheart, my wife Susan (yes, the same Susan
who slept in our closet while I tried to get my business
off the ground), on our first date in high school.

As we near the end of our lives, we must think of
our journey this way: how would you feel if at the end
of your road, you suddenly realize that you've been on

the wrong road? Or worse yet, that you were on the last stretch of your road. Granddad lived well and died broke. Yet, like Granddad, at the end of our road, we all come to the same end—we all die broke. The real question is, will we live well? While we have no choice in the matter of death, or when it will happen, we do have a choice in how we choose to live our lives. We can choose, right now, to use and enjoy our money. That's the true meaning of life.

Think about your life goals. Perhaps you want to fly to Peru, South America, in the next year instead of when you reach retirement age, when you may not be as physically able to climb Machu Picchu or even up a few stairs. You may dream of financially helping your grandchildren through college, but feel you shouldn't use your 401(k) money to do so because you've been told to avoid the fees and tax consequences of pulling out your money before retirement age.

The Live Well, Die Broke philosophy recognizes this reality. It embraces death by facing life. It recognizes that money is just a commodity, a tool to use to help us enjoy life during this brief stay on earth. Nothing more, nothing less.

Since I'm a full-time financial advisor, a fiduciary who has met with over 15,000 Savers in my lifetime, it would be beneficial to share, like Buddy Demling did with golf, the three financial keys to using and enjoying your money without the fear of it running out.

1. First, as you get older, move up to the next tee box. Put yourself in a position to use and enjoy this money while you can. Don't just let it sit there and grow because one day it might be too late for you to use and enjoy. Remember the husband whose wife lost her sight and how, although they had enough money for retirement, they couldn't go and enjoy the fruits of their labor. Position your money so that you can access some of it and use it while you still have your health and mobility.

2. Try to avoid the rough. You can shoot better golf when you keep the ball in the fairway. Same goes with your money. Taxes, fees, and risk all add up to playing from the rough. A well-trained financial advisor who understands retirement planning should be able to help you keep your money in the fairway.

3. Keep it simple. As you get older, why in the world would you want your money and your future to be filled with so many variables? There is no reason to make this stuff complicated. The financial world likes to confuse things because the hope is that you'll throw up your hands and keep the money with them. Remember, a dollar is not worth anything until it is converted to cash and used. Keeping things simple will allow you the freedom and confidence that you can do just that.

Life is short. Time passes quickly. The old Yiddish proverb, "We plan, God laughs," couldn't be truer in this sense. Regardless of how many barns you have or how big they are, no matter how much you have stockpiled in your 401(k), or the amount of Mailbox Money you receive each month . . . at the end of the road, we all die broke. Embracing this fact is the key to a worry-free life. I have found it to be quite liberating. The Live Well, Die Broke philosophy recognizes the temporary nature of life, and that you can't take anything with you.

The great writer and theologian Charles Spurgeon once had this to say about money: "Money is a funny thing: Those that have money worry with it; those who have none, worry without it."

This proves my point that money will not always allay your fears. Money, in and of itself, can actually produce more worries. Sure, I've been broke and I've had money. I'd rather have money and worry with it than have no money and worry without it. But still, money must be used as a temporary tool to do temporary things on this earth.

To enjoy a worry-free retirement, I've learned that one must have a sense of urgency for enjoying today, while at the same time, an understanding of the importance of planning for tomorrow. Retirement may seem like an inevitable part of your life, but it doesn't have to be the typical stepping away from your work. My view of retirement may not be your view of retirement. That's the beauty of it. The goal here is to truly be about stepping into your true desires, your hopes, your dreams, and not allow the circumstances of life, no matter how sometimes joyful or hard they might be, to dictate your future. I give God all the credit, as He has instilled in me a hope in my future that I declare will not be based on my past. The unique experiences of my past are past, yet the things in my future are yet to be seen. That's the cool part of this life. I hope this very reality is something that excites you rather than breeds fear and worry in you.

What road are you on? Are you on a road of worry and fear about the future? Are you afraid of getting off your wallet and doing the things you really want to do? Do you really think you're going to live forever or that you can take this stuff with you? Here's my suggestion: change your view about money. Begin to approach life as a temporary walk in the park, one that can and certainly should be enjoyed, but that will certainly one day come to an end, sometimes sooner than you think. Remember that life is too short to eat cheap bacon.

Change your view on money, right now. Quit worrying so much about it. Don't be afraid to use and enjoy it while you can, and for goodness' sake, don't rule out securing some Mailbox Money just like Granddad, so that one day you won't run out of it.

While you're changing your views about money, also change your views about what retirement can look like for you. Remember how I never envisioned myself retiring in the traditional sense and going off to play golf into the proverbial sunset? That kind of life just isn't for me.

It doesn't have to be for you either, unless that's your dream. Perhaps going to work each morning is fulfilling and keeps you going in life. Susan, as I mentioned, has been a nurse for most of her life and still works as a nurse, although she now focuses on a particular part of medicine that brings her joy and also allows her to work closely with people who need the most care.

The *Live Well, Die Broke* philosophy puts money in perspective because the good news is you are still alive, otherwise you wouldn't be reading this book. That means you have choices as to how you live the remainder of your life and what you do with your money. There is no right or wrong answer here. Regardless of whether you have one dollar or one million dollars, all roads lead to dying broke.

You see, the realization of life one day coming to a close is what puts our life—and our money—in perspective. There are too many people who come to the end of their road only to realize that life is not always about money and money is not always about life. While life and money must coexist, in the end, regardless of whether you're rich or broke, we all end up dead broke. The barns we build for the future are no more guaranteed to provide us use and enjoyment then, so much as they can today. While we must certainly plan for tomorrow, we must also learn to live for today. The perfect financial plan for one person, in terms of how they invest and spend their money, may not be for everyone.

Take a look at the next few pages that depict and explain my personal **Live Well, Die Broke** gameplan. It may connect the dots of what you've learned in this book and help you design your own personal financial plan. Again, there is no right or wrong answer to the philosophy of *Live Well, Die Broke*. That's the beauty of creating your own outlook on money and life. It's your money and your decision as to how you are going to spend it.

Tony's Personal Financial GamePlan to Live Well, Die Broke

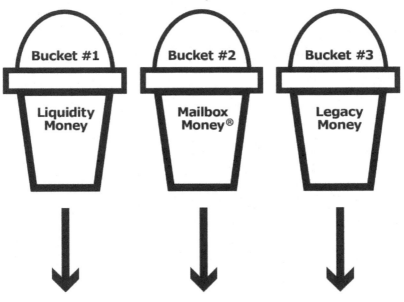

Bucket #1	Bucket #2	Bucket #3
Liquidity Money	**Mailbox Money®**	**Legacy Money**

✔ Bank Deposits	✔ Annuities	✔ Tax-free Assets
✔ Brokerage Accounts	✔ Social Security	✔ Life Insurance
✔ Insurance Contracts	✔ Real Estate Income	✔ Real Estate

My hope for you, as it has been in my own family, is to enjoy your money and the time you spend with your family, because in the end, that's the best way to live. My personal *Live Well, Die Broke* philosophy includes three different pots or "buckets" of money.

Bucket #1 includes money that I know for certain I can get access to when I need it; preferably with little or no hassle or penalties to do so. The investments I've placed inside this bucket provide the necessary liquidity and diversification – with very little risk to principal – whenever I need it. This bucket allows me to sleep better at night, knowing that if something unexpected arises, I have the funds to cover it.

Bucket #2 is my favorite bucket, Mailbox Money for life. Currently, this includes fixed annuities that provide me and my wife a guaranteed income in our later years, money that we will never outlive. Did I say "guaranteed?" As well, my commercial real estate provides a nice stream of income as well. And of course, since I am confident that social security will be around in some form or fashion, which is another form of Mailbox Money, we will enjoy a steady stream of income for the rest of our lives.

Bucket #3 In a perfect world, Susan and I will drain buckets one and two over our lifetime and then leave bucket number three to our kids. Bucket number three includes "tax-free" money that our kids can enjoy after we're dead and gone. Just like my Granddad, our mailbox money will end when we die. The assets in bucket three spring into action then. Without bucket three, our kids may be left with nothing.

Since I would like to leave them something without affecting our income, I have secured permanent life insurance and other assets to leave them when we die, assets that will pass to our kids without taxes! In other words, Susan and I can spend and enjoy all of our money and still leave tax-free, cold-hard cash to our kids. We die broke, but our kids receive the legacy we want them to have.

Mind you, this is my personal plan. Whether you wish to follow something similar to this is your call. That's the beauty of the *Live Well, Die Broke* philosophy on money and life...We all get to choose what we want to do for living, how much we wish to save, how we wish to spend our savings, and ultimately, if we'd like to leave a legacy when we're dead and gone.

If you need help sorting all this out, find and work with a trained retirement planning specialist who is a fiduciary and works with many different types of financial tools, not just one or two.

*Life is not about how much money
you accumulate over your lifetime;
but rather, how much you spend and
enjoy of what you have accumulated
during your lifetime.*

— **Tony Walker**

ABOUT THE AUTHOR

A native of Kentucky, Tony Walker is known by his friends, family and clients as a straight-shooting, down-to-earth guy. Throughout the financial services industry he's considered a true innovator in the field of retirement planning. A six-time author and host of his own TV show for more than twenty years, Tony's knack for keeping things simple has allowed him to personally help thousands of Savers better understand their options on how to better use, enjoy and protect their money. As Tony likes to say, "If I can help Savers worry less about money by showing them how to better use and enjoy it, then I've accomplished my mission in life."

To learn more about Tony's unique take on life and money, check out these books from Tony:

- The Worryfree Retirement – on Amazon and Barnes & Noble

- (Don't) Follow the Herd – on Amazon and Barnes & Noble

- The 3 Personalities of Money – on Amazon and Barnes & Noble

Access these free resources:

The Annuity Decision Guide for Savers and Mailbox Money for Life. Go to https://livewelldiebroke.com/adg/.

Want to learn how to invest based on your unique financial personality? Check out www.3personalities.com and take the free 5-minute test.

Made in USA - Kendallville, IN
92504_9781734426700
05.20.2022 1200